Leadership For Women Resilient & Ready

Empowering Women to Lead With Confidence and Success

Jess Pryce

Jessop Independent Publishers
ELEVATING MINDS, ENRICHING LIVES

© Copyright 2024 - All rights reserved.

The content contained within this book may not be reproduced, duplicated or transmitted without direct written permission from the author or the publisher.

Under no circumstances will any blame or legal responsibility be held against the publisher, or author, for any damages, reparation, or monetary loss due to the information contained within this book, either directly or indirectly.

Legal Notice:

This book is copyright protected. It is only for personal use. You cannot amend, distribute, sell, use, quote or paraphrase any part, or the content within this book, without the consent of the author or publisher.

Disclaimer Notice:

Please note the information contained within this document is for educational and entertainment purposes only. All effort has been executed to present accurate, up to date, reliable, complete information. No warranties of any kind are declared or implied. Readers acknowledge that the author is not engaged in the rendering of legal, financial, medical or professional advice. The content within this book has been derived from various sources. Please consult a licensed professional before attempting any techniques outlined in this book.

By reading this document, the reader agrees that under no circumstances is the author responsible for any losses, direct or indirect, that are incurred as a result of the use of the information contained within this document, including, but not limited to, errors, omissions, or inaccuracies.

Table of Contents

INTRODUCTION 1

CHAPTER 1: INTRODUCTION TO WOMEN IN LEADERSHIP 5

   OVERVIEW OF CURRENT LANDSCAPE 5
      Analysis of Gender Representation in Leadership Positions 6
      Discussing the Impact of Diverse Leadership Teams 7
      Industries Where Women Are Making Significant Strides 7
   TRENDS IN FEMALE LEADERSHIP 8

CHAPTER 2: BUILDING CONFIDENCE AND OVERCOMING IMPOSTER SYNDROME 15

   RECOGNIZING IMPOSTER SYNDROME 15
      Signs of Imposter Syndrome 16
   TIPS TO OVERCOME IMPOSTER SYNDROME 20
      Shift Your Mindset 20
      Get Support 21
      Set Realistic Goals With Manageable Actions 21
      Be Kind to Yourself 21
      Self-Reflective 22
      Practice Mindfulness 22
      Never Stop Learning 22
      Create a Supportive Environment 22
   PRACTICAL CONFIDENCE-BUILDING TECHNIQUES 23
   THE ROLE OF MENTORSHIP 25
   ACKNOWLEDGE ACCOMPLISHMENTS 27
   FINAL THOUGHTS 29

CHAPTER 3: LEVERAGING UNIQUE LEADERSHIP QUALITIES 31

   IDENTIFYING UNIQUE TRAITS 32
   ENHANCING EMOTIONAL INTELLIGENCE 35
      Self-Reflection and Awareness 35
      Active Listening 36
      Creating a Supportive and Inclusive Environment 36
      Recognizing and Managing Biases 37
      How High Emotional Intelligence (EQ) Can Propel Your Career 38
   UTILIZING EMPATHY IN LEADERSHIP 40
   FINAL INSIGHTS 42

CHAPTER 4: NETWORKING AND BUILDING SUPPORTIVE RELATIONSHIPS 44

IMPORTANCE OF NETWORKING 44
EFFECTIVE NETWORKING STRATEGIES..46
BUILDING ALLIANCES 49
  Strategic Partnerships *49*
MENTORSHIP AND SPONSORSHIP 51
FINAL THOUGHTS 52

CHAPTER 5: NAVIGATING GENDER BIAS AND STEREOTYPES........................... 55

RECOGNIZING BIASES...56
  Understanding Implicit Bias..*56*
  Why Understanding Implicit Bias Matters *56*
  Taking Action Against Implicit Bias *57*
  Monitoring Progress...*58*
ADVOCACY STRATEGIES 59
HANDLING DIFFICULT SITUATIONS 61
  Conflict Resolution Strategies..*61*
  Emotional Regulation Techniques *62*
  Cultural Intelligence..*63*
  Communication Skills..*64*
CLOSING REMARKS 65

CHAPTER 6: DEVELOPING RESILIENCE AND ADAPTABILITY 67

CULTIVATING A GROWTH MINDSET 67
STRESS MANAGEMENT TECHNIQUES..70
  Practicing Mindfulness and Meditation *70*
  Engaging in Regular Physical Exercise..*71*
  Establishing Boundaries for Work-Life Harmony......................................*72*
  Seeking Support Networks and Resources..*75*
LEARNING FROM FAILURES 75
MAINTAINING WORK-LIFE BALANCE 77
  Setting Priorities and Boundaries *77*
  Scheduling Self-Care Activities...*79*
  Delegating Responsibilities and Empowering Others...............................*80*
  Establishing Healthy Habits and Routines *80*
SUMMARY AND REFLECTIONS 81

CHAPTER 7: MASTERING COMMUNICATION SKILLS... 83

VERBAL AND NON-VERBAL COMMUNICATION 83
  Understanding Body Language *84*
  Utilizing Body Language to Convey Confidence and Authority *84*
  Tailoring Communication Style to Resonate With Diverse Audiences..........*85*

Utilizing Active Listening to Foster Understanding and Collaboration 85
  Practical Guidelines for Enhancing Non-Verbal Communication............... 86
  NEGOTIATION SKILLS... 87
    Preparation for Negotiations... 87
    Managing Conflict and Reaching Mutually Beneficial Agreements 88
    Overcoming Gender Biases in Negotiation Settings 88
    Leveraging Emotional Intelligence for Successful Negotiation Outcomes... 89
    Practice, Practice, Practice 90
  PUBLIC SPEAKING TIPS 91
  CONCLUDING THOUGHTS.. 92

CHAPTER 8: VISIONARY LEADERSHIP..**94**

  CRAFTING A COMPELLING VISION 94
  STRATEGIC PLANNING 96
  INSPIRING AND MOTIVATING TEAMS... 98
    Embracing a Transformational Leadership Style 98
    Celebrating Achievements and Milestones... 99
    Cultivating a Supportive and Inclusive Work Environment...................... 100
  INNOVATIVE THINKING 100
  BRINGING IT ALL TOGETHER 102

CHAPTER 9: DELEGATION AND TRUST-BUILDING **104**

  IMPORTANCE OF DELEGATION... 104
  TECHNIQUES FOR EFFECTIVE DELEGATION 107
    Task Analysis: Matching Tasks to Team Members 107
    Clear Instructions: Setting Your Team Up for Success 107
    Regular Check-ins: Keeping Communication Open.................................. 108
    Feedback Loop: Ensuring Completion to Satisfaction.............................. 109
  BUILDING TRUST WITH YOUR TEAM 109
  FOSTERING ACCOUNTABILITY... 112
    Setting Expectations 112
    Feedback Mechanisms.. 112
    Recognition of Efforts 113
    Learning From Mistakes 113
    Creating a Culture of Accountability... 114
  BRINGING IT ALL TOGETHER 114

CHAPTER 10: LIFELONG LEARNING AND CONTINUOUS   IMPROVEMENT
....**117**

  EMBRACING CONTINUOUS EDUCATION 117
  SEEKING FEEDBACK FOR GROWTH 119
  STAYING CURRENT WITH INDUSTRY TRENDS.. 120
  PERSONAL DEVELOPMENT STRATEGIES 121
  FINAL THOUGHTS 122

CONCLUSION 125

REFERENCES 127

ABOUT THE AUTHOR 140

ADDITIONAL BOOKS BY THIS AUTHOR 142

Introduction

When you think about leadership, what comes to mind? Perhaps it's the image of a commanding CEO steering a corporation through turbulent waters. Maybe it's a visionary entrepreneur turning ingenious ideas into thriving enterprises. Now, what if these leaders were women? How might their unique perspectives and strengths redefine society's understanding of leadership and innovation?

This book is crafted for women like you—women who aspire to break new ground in corporate settings or lead successful businesses. Whether you're climbing the corporate ladder or nurturing your own entrepreneurial dream, the challenges and opportunities you face are distinct. Female leaders bring invaluable qualities to the table, an array of skills and insights that can significantly influence organizational culture, decision-making processes, and ultimately, success.

Female leadership isn't just about occupying executive positions; it's about reshaping how we perceive leadership itself. Women often have a different approach, one that involves collaboration, empathy, and a holistic view of the workplace and marketplace. These attributes aren't just beneficial, they're essential in today's interconnected and rapidly evolving world. As women rise to leadership roles, they infuse organizations with a diversity of thought, promoting more innovative and inclusive environments. By bringing together varied perspectives, female leaders drive creativity and problem-solving, enhancing teams' ability to navigate complex challenges.

Take emotional intelligence, for example. Emotional intelligence refers to the ability to understand and manage both your own emotions and those of others. It's a vital skill for any leader, but it's especially powerful in the hands of women. We're naturally attuned to the nuances of human emotion, and this means we're are adept at navigating interpersonal dynamics. This emotional acumen translates into better communication, conflict resolution, and overall team cohesion. When leaders harness emotional intelligence, they foster environments where employees feel valued and understood, leading to higher morale and productivity. Navigating the path to leadership as a woman presents its own set of hurdles and achievements. From breaking through the proverbial glass ceiling to balancing professional aspirations with personal commitments, the journey is layered with unique experiences.

However, these challenges should be viewed not as impediments but as stepping stones that hone your resilience, fortitude, and adaptability. Each obstacle overcome adds to your arsenal of skills, making you an even more formidable leader.

Like many women, I faced immense criticism early in my career. Instead of backing down, I used it as fuel to improve and showcase my abilities. Each criticism offered me a chance to enhance my skills and prove myself even more in the competitive corporate world.

For instance, despite encountering gender bias in the workplace, I saw it as a chance to demonstrate that capability knows no gender. This attitude helped me excel in more challenging roles, which led to my advancement up the corporate ladder.

Don't get me wrong, it wasn't always smooth sailing. Once, a major project I was leading faced one setback after the other. My ability to adapt, however, helped me turn these setbacks into stepping stones, leading to a successful result and a promotion.

That is why I decided to write this book. I want to help women navigate the multifaceted nature of female leadership. I want to give you strategies to develop and harness your emotional intelligence, tips for building and sustaining robust relationships, and methods for mastering the art of delegation.

Through the chapters ahead, real-life stories and practical advice will guide you, providing a roadmap to help you navigate your leadership journey with confidence and optimism. We will delve into the ways female leaders have historically transformed industries, led to significant societal changes, and driven by economic growth. Their experiences offer valuable lessons and serve as beacons of inspiration for aspiring leaders. Additionally, you will gain insight into how to cultivate a leadership style that resonates with your values and leverages your unique strengths. I also want you to start to see every failure as an opportunity to learn to check and adjust. View failures, not as a defeat, but as a way to grow and become a better leader. I have failed as a leader many times and have been disappointed with the decisions and behaviors I have displayed. I have used these as learning opportunities to change my leadership style and behaviors to be more satisfying for me and my team.

As you read, remember that leadership is not a solitary endeavor. It's about inspiring and elevating those around you. By embracing your authentic self and recognizing the value you bring, you'll be better equipped to lead with purpose and impact. This book is not just a guide; it's a companion on your journey, offering support and encouragement along the way.

Female leadership is indispensable in today's world. Your perspective, emotional intelligence, relationship-building abilities, and delegation skills are crucial assets that can transform organizations and drive substantial progress. Embrace the challenges, celebrate the victories, and continue to strive for excellence. The future of leadership is bright, and it includes brilliant, capable women like you, ready to make a lasting difference. Welcome to the next chapter of your leadership journey.

Chapter 1:

Introduction to Women in Leadership

The only safe ship in a storm is leadership. –Faye Wattleton

Understanding the complexities of women in leadership roles is essential for grasping the challenges we face in climbing the corporate ladder. This chapter delves into the present environment where women navigate both obstacles and opportunities in leadership positions. One thing is certain, women bring distinct strengths to leadership roles, such as excellent communication skills and the enhanced ability to handle crises. By examining the dynamics of female leadership, you will gain valuable insights into how diverse leadership teams enhance decision-making and drive innovation within organizations. In this chapter, you'll find an in-depth analysis of gender representation in leadership positions, highlighting ongoing disparities and the pronounced underrepresentation of women in top executive roles. The discussion will explore how these disparities affect organizational performance and culture, emphasizing the positive impact that diverse teams can have on a company's success. Additionally, the chapter identifies industries where women are making significant strides, such as technology, healthcare, and the nonprofit sector. Through examining these examples, you will understand the broader trends shaping women's leadership roles today and appreciate the ongoing efforts to foster more inclusive and equitable workplaces.

Overview of Current Landscape

Providing insights into the current environment for women in leadership roles involves a nuanced understanding of the various factors shaping these dynamics. Let's delve into the analysis of gender representation in leadership positions, highlight disparities in gender distribution within management and executive roles, discuss the impact of diverse leadership teams on organizational performance, and identify industries where women are making significant strides.

Analysis of Gender Representation in Leadership Positions

In recent years, there's been an increased focus on the representation of women in leadership roles within the corporate world. Despite progress, the status quo reveals that women remain underrepresented in top executive positions. For example, while women make up nearly half of the workforce, they hold only about 35% of senior management positions (Ariella, 2023). According to one study, hiring a demographically diverse workforce boosts financial performance, indicating that varied teams lead to better problem-solving and overall performance (Elias, 2018).

The underrepresentation of women in leadership is not just a numbers game; it has far-reaching implications. Women bring essential qualities such as heightened emotional intelligence, persuasiveness, and a sharp sense of awareness to the workplace, as well as empathy, collaboration, and relationship-building. When the strengths of a diverse team are combined, organizations can achieve enhanced decision-making and innovative solutions (Elias, 2018).

Highlighting Disparities in Gender Distribution

At your next meeting, have a look around the room. How many women do you see? Better yet, how many women in leadership positions are in attendance? Disparities in gender distribution within management and executive roles are stark. Fortune 500 companies with the highest representation of women board directors had higher financial performance on average than those with the lowest representation (Catalyst, 2022). Despite this, only 4.4 percent of 500 companies employed female CEOs. Additionally, full-time working women earned just 83 percent of what their male counterparts did (Elias, 2018). This indicates a significant pay gap that persists even at the highest organizational levels. These disparities are influenced by various factors. Cultural biases and stereotypes often play a crucial role in limiting women's access to leadership opportunities. Unfortunately, we're frequently perceived as less competent or less committed due to societal expectations around gender roles. Consequently, we have to work harder to prove our capabilities and overcome implicit biases in the workplace.

Discussing the Impact of Diverse Leadership Teams

Evidence consistently shows that diverse leadership teams positively impact organizational performance. Diverse teams bring varied perspectives, which foster creativity and innovation. They are also better equipped to understand and respond to the needs of a diverse customer base. Companies in the top quartile for gender diversity on executive teams were 21 percent more likely to outperform on profitability compared to those in the bottom quartile (Dixon-Fyle, 2019). Moreover, diverse leadership teams contribute to higher employee satisfaction and retention rates. Employees tend to feel more valued and understood in inclusive environments, leading to increased engagement and reduced turnover. This, in turn, enhances overall organizational efficiency and competitiveness.

Industries Where Women Are Making Significant Strides

While challenges persist across many sectors, some industries are showing promising progress in promoting women to leadership roles. For instance, the technology sector, traditionally male-dominated, is witnessing a gradual increase in women's representation at the helm of companies. Initiatives aimed at encouraging girls to pursue STEM (Science, Technology, Engineering, Mathematics) education and careers are beginning to multiply. Similarly, the healthcare industry has seen notable advancements. Women now occupy a significant portion of leadership positions in hospitals, pharmaceutical companies, and health-related research institutions.

In fact, women make up 70 percent of the global health workforce, although they hold only about 25 percent of global health leadership roles (Harrison et al., 2022). Another industry where women are making substantial gains is the nonprofit sector. Organizations focusing on social justice, community development, and environmental sustainability often have women in key leadership positions. These roles allow women to leverage their collaborative and empathetic strengths to drive impactful change.

Trends in Female Leadership

Exploring recent developments in women's participation in leadership roles reveals a landscape of evolving perceptions, contrasting regional progress, successful initiatives, and the rise of women-led ventures. This exploration helps us understand the dynamic shifts currently taking place. It offers insight into how these changes can be applied to further empower women, such as yourself, aspiring to, or those who are already in leadership positions.

The perception of women in leadership roles has seen a significant transformation over recent years. Traditional gender stereotypes that once restricted women's access to leadership have started to break down, replaced by a growing acceptance of women as capable and effective leaders. This shift is partly driven by an increasing awareness of the benefits that diverse leadership brings to organizational success. Studies show that companies with higher female representation in leadership tend to perform better financially, foster more innovative solutions, and maintain healthier work environments.

However, despite these positive trends, women still face unique challenges such as unconscious bias and balancing professional and personal responsibilities, which continue to hinder their full participation in leadership roles. As a mother, I know how difficult it is to manage being a wife and mother while also trying to pursue a career. There were times when I truly felt it was an impossible task. It was expected that I take care of my children, clean the house, and go to work—all without getting tired and forever with a smile on my face.

I had to have a long chat with my husband about dividing responsibilities in a more equal manner and even hiring help, like a housecleaner or a landscaping company. This just shows how ingrained the "female caregiver and homemaker" stereotype is that even those who love you need to be guided out of that way of thinking. Thankfully, I have a partner who is very supportive of my career and understands that I'm more than *just a wife and mother*—I'm an intelligent and driven woman with lofty career ambitions.

When contrasting the progress made in Western countries versus emerging markets, there are notable differences in the pace and nature of advancements. In many Western nations, legislative measures and corporate policies have been implemented to support gender equality in leadership. For instance, several European countries have introduced quotas requiring a certain percentage of board positions to be held by women.

These efforts have led to a gradual increase in female representation at the highest levels of management. On the other hand, emerging markets often face different sets of barriers, including cultural norms, socio-economic constraints, and limited access to education for women. Nevertheless, there are countries in which positive changes are happening. For example, Rwanda boasts one of the highest percentages of women in parliament globally, demonstrating that with the right policies and societal support, substantial progress is possible regardless of economic status (UN Women, 2023). This is very exciting for future generations.

Internationally, several initiatives have successfully promoted women in leadership roles, serving as models for other regions to emulate. The HeForShe (n.d.) campaign by UN Women is a prime example, encouraging men to advocate for gender equality and support women's leadership. Additionally, various global networks like the Women's Empowerment Principles (WEPs) (n.d.) provide guidelines for businesses to promote gender equality in the workplace actively. Governmental policies like parental leave and subsidized childcare also play a critical role in enabling women to balance leadership responsibilities and family life. In Norway, for instance, the presence of women in municipal councils has been directly linked to improved childcare coverage, showcasing the practical impacts of inclusive policies (Chattopadhyay & Duflo, 2004). Women-led initiatives and entrepreneurial ventures have also risen significantly, contributing to economic growth and innovation. These initiatives not only create opportunities for women to start and grow their businesses but also challenge traditional business models and encourage inclusive entrepreneurship. Moreover, as more women step into entrepreneurial roles, they pave the way for future generations by breaking down barriers and serving as role models. For instance, sectors like technology and finance, traditionally male-dominated, are seeing more women launching startups, thus gradually transforming the industry landscapes (World Economic Forum, 2022).

The journey of women in leadership has been marked by significant milestones, shaped by pioneering figures and crucial moments in history. Examining this journey not only provides a deeper understanding of the progress made but also highlights the persistent challenges that women have faced and continue to overcome in their quest for equality in leadership roles. Seeing successful women gave me hope in my earlier days and inspired me to keep going through the most difficult circumstances.

One of the most pivotal figures in the early fight for women's rights was Abigail Adams. In a letter written to her husband, John Adams, in 1776, she implored him and his fellow members of the Continental Congress to "remember the ladies" and ensure that new laws were more favorable to women (American Battlefield Trust, n.d.). This plea set the stage for a broader movement advocating for women's rights.

Moving forward to the mid-19th century, the Seneca Falls Convention of 1848 marked a watershed moment in women's rights. Organized by Elizabeth Cady Stanton and Lucretia Mott, this convention gathered activists to discuss the social, civil, and religious conditions and rights of women (Worthen, 2020). The Declaration of Sentiments, modeled after the Declaration of Independence, was drafted and signed, demanding equal rights for women, including the right to vote. This event ignited decades of activism and laid the groundwork for future advancements.

Sojourner Truth, an African American abolitionist and women's rights activist, further exemplified the determination of early female leaders. Her famous 1851 speech, *Ain't I a Woman?* delivered at the Ohio Women's Rights Convention, challenged prevailing notions of racial and gender inferiority by highlighting the intersectional struggles faced by black women. Truth's advocacy was instrumental in broadening the scope of the women's rights movement to include issues of race and class. Despite these significant efforts, early women leaders faced immense challenges. Suffragists like Susan B. Anthony and Elizabeth Cady Stanton encountered societal opposition, legal obstacles, and personal sacrifices. Anthony was famously arrested for voting illegally in the 1872 presidential election, illustrating the resistance women faced. These adversities, however, underscored the resilience and commitment of these trailblazers and amplified their impact on future generations.

The ratification of the 19th Amendment in 1920 marked a landmark moment in American history, granting women the right to vote after decades of suffrage activism. This victory was not just a triumph for voting rights but also a critical step toward achieving broader gender equality in societal participation and leadership. By securing the vote, women have gained a powerful tool to influence legislation and public policy, paving the way for greater representation in leadership positions across various sectors (Burkett, 2019).

Following the suffrage movement, the mid-20th century saw the rise of feminist leaders who championed women's rights on multiple fronts. Betty Friedan's publication of *The Feminine Mystique* in 1963 sparked a renewed interest in feminism, challenging the traditional roles assigned to women and advocating for their active participation in the workforce and leadership positions.

This period witnessed significant legislative achievements, such as the Equal Pay Act of 1963 and Title IX of the Education Amendments of 1972, which prohibited sex-based discrimination in federally funded education programs, thus promoting gender equality in educational opportunities and athletics (Burkett, 2019).

Another notable figure was Gloria Steinem, who emerged as a leading voice in the women's liberation movement during the 1960s and 70s. Steinem co-founded Ms. magazine, providing a platform for feminist ideas and advocacy. Her work emphasized the importance of women's autonomy, reproductive rights, and political representation, further advancing the agenda for gender equality.

Parallel to these achievements in the United States, international progress in women's leadership also gained momentum. Figures like Sirimavo Bandaranaike of Sri Lanka, who became the world's first female prime minister in 1960, and Indira Gandhi of India, who served as prime minister from 1966 to 1977 and again from 1980 until her assassination in 1984, demonstrated that women could hold top leadership positions traditionally dominated by men. Their tenures, though met with varying degrees of success and controversy, underscored the global shift toward recognizing women's potential in political leadership.

Despite these advances, examining historical obstacles reveals parallels with contemporary barriers. Today, women continue to face challenges such as gender bias, unequal pay, and underrepresentation in executive roles. The glass ceiling, a metaphorical barrier preventing women from reaching top leadership positions, remains a reality for many. However, historical context serves as a reminder of the progress made and the ongoing struggle for equality.

In modern contexts, many initiatives have brought attention to issues of sexual harassment and assault in the workplace, highlighting the persistent gendered obstacles women encounter. Additionally, the increasing emphasis on diversity and inclusion in corporate governance reflects a growing recognition of the value that women bring to leadership roles. Companies and organizations are increasingly implementing policies and practices aimed at fostering gender equity and creating supportive environments for female leaders.

Drawing from history, it is evident that the journey toward gender equality in leadership is ongoing. The legacies of early women leaders serve as both inspiration and a call to action for contemporary female leaders to continue advocating for equal opportunities and representation. By understanding the historical context, aspiring women leaders can appreciate the sacrifices and triumphs of those who came before them and draw strength from their enduring legacy. As we look toward the future, it is essential to continue challenging systemic barriers and advocating for policies that support women's advancement in leadership roles. This includes addressing issues such as gender pay gaps, providing mentorship and sponsorship opportunities for women, and promoting work-life balance through flexible work arrangements and parental leave policies. In this chapter, we explored the unique challenges and opportunities that women face in leadership roles. We examined the current landscape of gender representation, highlighting both progress and persistent disparities within various industries. Key insights into how diverse leadership teams positively impact organizational performance were discussed, emphasizing the value women bring to the table with their distinct qualities and perspectives.

Additionally, we identified sectors where women are making significant strides, showcasing promising advancements in technology, healthcare, and nonprofit organizations. As we move forward, it's clear that while there have been significant improvements, there's still much work to be done to achieve true gender parity in leadership. Addressing cultural biases, supporting women's professional development, and fostering inclusive work environments are critical steps in this journey.

By learning from successful initiatives and drawing inspiration from pioneering women leaders, we can create a more equitable landscape where women not only aspire to leadership but thrive in those roles. This ongoing effort will not only benefit women but also drive innovation and success across all levels of business and society.

In the coming chapter, we're going to look at how to overcome self-doubt and fear. We'll discuss imposter syndrome and the fear many women face of being exposed as frauds despite excelling at their careers. This is a valuable chapter to boost your confidence, so you can go out there and show the world what you can do without doubting yourself!

Chapter 2:
Building Confidence and Overcoming Imposter Syndrome

You gain strength, courage and confidence by every experience in which you really stop to look fear in the face. –Eleanor Roosevelt

Many people in leadership positions face self-doubt and fear of being exposed as frauds, despite their accomplishments. This chapter delves into effective strategies to combat these feelings and bolster self-confidence, allowing women to thrive professionally and personally.

Throughout this chapter, we'll explore a variety of techniques designed to develop confidence and tips to overcome imposter syndrome. Practical approaches such as setting realistic goals, celebrating milestones, and building a strong support system are discussed in detail. Additionally, the chapter highlights the importance of self-compassion, reflection, and mindfulness practices in maintaining emotional well-being. By adopting these strategies, you'll be able to transform self-doubt into a powerful force for growth and success.

Recognizing Imposter Syndrome

Imposter syndrome is a common struggle among women leaders, manifesting as persistent doubts about one's abilities and accomplishments. Despite their success, many leaders feel unworthy, attributing achievements to luck rather than competence. This phenomenon can have profound psychological effects, such as anxiety and depression. Imposter syndrome often causes individuals to constantly fear exposure to fraud, which can be mentally exhausting. The impact of imposter syndrome on career advancement and confidence is significant. If you experience these feelings, you may be hesitant to pursue promotions or new opportunities, doubting your qualifications. You may overprepare for tasks, fearing mistakes, which leads to burnout. The constant self-doubt hinders assertiveness in meetings and negotiations, affecting your professional growth. These patterns create a vicious cycle, where a lack of confidence hampers performance, reinforcing the belief of inadequacy.

Signs of Imposter Syndrome

Understanding that the path to overcoming imposter syndrome is ongoing will empower you to embrace your journey. You need to learn to appreciate your progress, no matter how small, and recognize your value in the workplace. Recognizing the signs and behaviors associated with imposter syndrome is crucial. By identifying these patterns, you can begin to address the root causes of your self-doubt.

Perfectionism

Perfectionism is when someone wants everything to be just right, perfect, with no mistakes. This can lead to a lot of stress. You might feel anxious because you think you must always meet high standards. This pressure can make you reluctant to try new things. You might avoid tasks that you fear won't turn out perfectly, missing out on opportunities to learn and grow. Instead of enjoying the process, you focus solely on the end result. You think, *If it's not perfect, it's not good enough.* People with imposter syndrome often feel this way. They believe that whatever they do is never good enough, even if others say it's great. So, they keep trying to make things better, but they still don't feel satisfied.

> **Success Strategy**: Create a guide for self-reflection you can use to overcome possible fear of failure. Write down your fears but next to it include past experiences that's proof that you have nothing to fear. For example, if you have a fear of speaking in front of people, think back to a time where you successfully gave a presentation.

Self-Sabotage

Self-sabotage is when someone stops themselves from doing something because they are scared of failing. For instance, a woman with imposter syndrome might not apply for a job because she thinks she won't get it anyway. This fear of failing holds her back and stops her from taking on new challenges.

> **Success Strategy**: Set realistic and achievable short-term goals. This will help you maintain motivation and provide a clear path toward achieving your longer-term objectives.

Comparing and Dismissing Compliments

When someone compares themselves to others all the time and always feels like they don't measure up, it can be a sign of imposter syndrome. When you feel like an impostor, self-deprecating comments often follow. You might say, *I just got lucky*, or, *I don't deserve this*, even when your hard work is clear to everyone else. These thoughts create a cycle of doubt that is hard to break. Friends might say, "You're doing great!" but the words don't stick. Instead, you focus on the one comment that points out a mistake. The feeling of being a fraud lingers, overshadowing your accomplishments. Also, when you don't believe the compliments you receive, thinking that others are just being nice and don't really mean it, it shows a lack of self-confidence.

> **Success Strategy**: Create a compliment culture within your team. Think of strategies for building an environment that encourages giving and receiving compliments. This will make it easier for you to be more accepting when people say good things about you.

Addressing Imposter Syndrome

Understanding these signs and behaviors is important for women to start dealing with imposter syndrome. By recognizing these patterns in themselves, they can begin to figure out why they doubt themselves.

It's essential to identify these feelings and work on building self-esteem and confidence, so they can stop feeling like they are imposters and start believing in themselves.

Samantha's Story

I was a software engineer at a prestigious tech company. Although I was surrounded by brilliant minds and working on cutting-edge projects, it's still a very male-dominated industry. There was this persistent voice whispering in my ear, telling me that I didn't belong. *They'll find out you're a fraud—just a lucky imposter who stumbled into this position.*

This voice had been haunting me since I first started my career and led to increased levels of anxiety. I found myself questioning every accomplishment and magnifying every mistake. Feeling like an impostor held me back from taking risks, speaking up in meetings, and from truly believing in myself.

The turning point came during a particularly stressful project. I was assigned to lead a team of developers, and the pressure was immense. The voice in my head screamed *You're not capable. You'll fail. Everyone will see you for the impostor you are.* But this time, I decided to fight back. I reminded myself of my skills, my experience, and the positive feedback I had received from colleagues. I focused on the task at hand, breaking it down into manageable steps and seeking help when needed. It wasn't easy.

The feeling that I didn't belong continued, but I learned to counter it with positive affirmations and treating myself with compassion. On top of that, I started celebrating small wins—focusing on my progress rather than what I perceived as shortcomings.

The project was a success. My team delivered on time and exceeded expectations. The imposter syndrome didn't vanish overnight, but its grip on me loosened. I learned to recognize its patterns and challenge its negativity. I surrounded myself with supportive colleagues who believed in me, and I sought out mentors who offered guidance and encouragement.

Today, I still have moments of self-doubt, but I no longer let them define me. I am a capable and valuable member of my team, and I am proud of the work I do. The journey to overcome imposter syndrome is ongoing, but with each step, I gain more confidence and self-belief.

> I share my story not to claim victory, but to offer hope to other women struggling with the same invisible enemy. You are not alone. You are capable. And you are worthy.

Tips to Overcome Imposter Syndrome

When navigating your journey as a leader, remember that you are part of a supportive team. Your promotion was earned through the confidence that your supervisor has in your abilities. It's important to recognize that you are not expected to possess all the knowledge right away. Don't hesitate to seek clarification and solicit feedback. Your contributions matter and collaboration is key. Here are some strategies to help you tackle feelings of imposter syndrome.

Shift Your Mindset

Developing a growth mindset is a powerful strategy to overcome self-limiting beliefs. A growth mindset refers to the belief that abilities and intelligence can be developed through dedication and hard work. This concept, popularized by psychologist Carol Dweck, contrasts with a fixed mindset, which holds that our qualities are carved in stone and cannot change.

There are apps that will provide you with three to 10 quick tips on anything you need to learn more about. Engaging in such an activity is a great way to expand your mind. Of course, attending workshops and reading are tried-and-tested methods to develop your mind. A growth mindset also involves viewing failures as learning opportunities rather than proof of inadequacy.

Adopting this mindset helps shift focus from fixed traits to the potential for growth and improvement. For instance, instead of thinking, I'm not good at public speaking, you should think, I can improve my public speaking skills with practice. This positive outlook encourages resilience and perseverance.

Get Support

Building a support system is another effective way to combat imposter syndrome. Connecting with mentors, peers, and coaches can provide valuable feedback and encouragement. Sharing experiences with others who have faced similar challenges fosters a sense of community and reduces feelings of isolation.

Moreover, seeking mentorship from experienced leaders who have overcome imposter syndrome offers practical insights and strategies for managing it. I don't know where I'd be without strong mentors walking by my side, encouraging me when I thought I couldn't do it.

Set Realistic Goals With Manageable Actions

Another practical approach is setting realistic goals and celebrating achieved milestones. Breaking down larger objectives into manageable steps makes progress more visible and attainable. Acknowledging incremental successes reinforces self-worth and motivation. For example, if you successfully complete a project, recognizing this accomplishment will boost your confidence to tackle future challenges.

Be Kind to Yourself

Practicing self-compassion is essential in addressing imposter syndrome. As a female leader, you must learn to treat yourself with kindness and understanding, especially during setbacks. This means reframing negative self-talk and forgiving mistakes instead of dwelling on them.

Self-compassion fosters a healthier relationship with oneself, promoting emotional well-being and reducing stress.

Self-Reflective

Engaging in regular reflection can help you gain perspective on your accomplishments and capabilities. Keeping a journal to document successes, challenges, and lessons learned can be empowering.

Reflecting on past achievements serves as a reminder of one's competencies and growth over time. This practice can counteract the tendency to forget or minimize successes, which is common in those experiencing imposter syndrome.

Practice Mindfulness

Incorporating mindfulness techniques, such as meditation and deep breathing exercises, can also mitigate the effects of imposter syndrome. Mindfulness practices help you stay present and grounded, reducing anxiety about future performance and past mistakes. By fostering a sense of calm and focus, these techniques enable women leaders to approach their roles with greater clarity and confidence.

Never Stop Learning

Educating oneself about imposter syndrome is another crucial step. Understanding its origins and prevalence demystifies the experience, making it easier to manage. Reading books, attending workshops, and following thought leaders on the subject equip women with knowledge and tools to combat imposter syndrome effectively.

Create a Supportive Environment

Advocating for a supportive workplace culture that acknowledges and addresses imposter syndrome benefits everyone. Organizations can implement training programs and workshops to raise awareness and provide strategies for managing imposter syndrome. Encouraging an environment where open discussions about self-doubt are welcomed helps reduce stigma and promotes collective growth.

Practical Confidence-Building Techniques

When stepping into leadership roles, especially as women, it is crucial to build and show confidence. One of the most effective methods for increasing confidence is through the power of visualization. Visualization involves mentally picturing your success and desired outcomes, which can significantly boost your confidence and performance. Imagine yourself successfully leading a meeting or achieving a major milestone in your career. By consistently creating these mental images of success, you can begin to internalize them, making them feel more attainable and realistic.

Practicing positive affirmations complements visualization by reinforcing a confident mindset. Positive affirmations are statements that you repeat to yourself to build self-belief and counter negative thoughts. For example, telling yourself, *I am a capable and effective leader* each morning can gradually shift your mindset toward greater self-confidence. It might seem simple, but these repeated affirmations can have a profound impact on how you perceive yourself and how others see you.

I write positive affirmations on little notes and stick them around my mirror. That way, whenever I'm brushing my teeth or washing my hands, I read them to boost my self-confidence. It may sound silly, but it really works! There were days when I wanted to quit my job, but when I got home and saw these messages, it encouraged me to keep at it.

Another actionable strategy is setting achievable goals and tracking your progress. Start with small, manageable objectives that you can realistically accomplish within a given time frame. Achieving these smaller goals will not only provide a sense of accomplishment but also pave the way for tackling larger, more challenging tasks. For instance, if you're working on improving your public speaking skills, set an initial goal to present at a small team meeting before progressing to larger audiences. By regularly tracking your progress and celebrating these incremental successes, you build a stronger foundation of self-assurance.

Taking calculated risks is another key component in building confidence. Stepping outside of your comfort zone can be intimidating, but it's necessary for growth. When you take risks, you expose yourself to new experiences and challenges, which can enhance your problem-solving abilities and resilience. It's important to understand that failure is a natural part of this process. Instead of fearing failure, always view it as a learning opportunity. Analyze what went wrong, extract valuable lessons from the experience, and apply them to future endeavors. This approach not only strengthens your confidence but also prepares you to tackle bigger challenges with a more resilient mindset.

Furthermore, creating a supportive environment that fosters constructive feedback and recognition can empower you in your leadership journey. Constructive criticism helps you identify areas for improvement while positive recognition reinforces your achievements and boosts your morale. Organizations can play a pivotal role in this by cultivating a culture where feedback is encouraged and recognition is commonplace (Mesquita, 2024). We will talk more about the significance of mentorship a little further down and you can expect me to mention the importance of having a support network many times because it's often a critical part of advancing your career that is overlooked.

Resilience is another crucial quality for women leaders striving to build confidence. Resilience enables you to manage stress, recover from setbacks, and stay focused on long-term goals. Developing resilience involves adopting a growth mindset, which means viewing challenges as opportunities to learn and grow, rather than insurmountable obstacles.

Wellness programs and emotional support are beneficial resources that organizations can offer to help develop resilience among their leaders and teams (Mesquita, 2024). To further strengthen confidence, it's essential to practice self-compassion and reframe negative self-talk. Being kind to yourself and understanding that everyone makes mistakes can significantly reduce feelings of self-doubt. When negative thoughts arise, challenge them by asking whether they are based on facts or merely assumptions. Replace these negative thoughts with positive, realistic ones. Whenever you feel that you're not good enough, remind yourself of past successes and the skills you bring to the table.

Finally, practicing effective communication is vital for building assertiveness in leadership roles. Effective communication involves expressing your thoughts, needs, and desires clearly and respectfully, without diminishing others. Techniques like active listening, backtracking to confirm understanding, and providing constructive feedback can enhance your communication skills (University of Minnesota, 2023). By being an effective communicator, you demonstrate confidence in your ideas while fostering a collaborative and respectful environment.

The Role of Mentorship

Understanding the significance of mentorship in building confidence and leadership skills is essential. Mentorship provides a robust support system, offering guidance and encouragement that can be instrumental in personal and professional growth. In this section, we will delve into the benefits of mentorship, how to build meaningful mentor-mentee relationships, identifying potential mentors, and seeking valuable feedback and advice.

Mentorship offers numerous benefits that are vital to leadership development. One of the core advantages is the guidance it provides. A mentor's experience can serve as a blueprint, helping mentees navigate their careers by avoiding common pitfalls and leveraging opportunities effectively. This support often translates into increased self-confidence and more informed decision-making.

The mentor's role is not just to provide answers but to empower mentees to think critically and develop problem-solving skills. According to research, having a mentor can significantly enhance career advancement by providing insights into industry trends and organizational dynamics (Elliot, 2023).

Building a strong mentor-mentee relationship is pivotal for the success of the mentorship process. Trust and respect are foundational elements in this relationship. Both parties should feel comfortable sharing their thoughts and experiences without judgment.

Mutual respect fosters an environment where constructive feedback can be given and received openly, furthering personal and professional development. It's also crucial for the mentorship to be a two-way street, where both the mentor and mentee learn from each other. This mutual learning ensures that the relationship remains dynamic and beneficial for both parties.

To establish trust, start with open communication. Clearly define expectations, goals, and boundaries at the beginning of the relationship. Regular check-ins and honest conversations about progress and challenges help in maintaining transparency. Respect also involves understanding and valuing each other's time and commitments. Ensuring that meetings are productive and focused shows respect for the mentor's contribution and the mentee's growth journey.

Identifying potential mentors who align with your personal and professional goals is crucial. Look for individuals who have achieved what you aspire to accomplish and whose values resonate with yours. They should have the expertise and experience relevant to your career path. Networking events, professional associations, and online platforms like LinkedIn are excellent resources for finding potential mentors. Additionally, look within your organization for leaders who exemplify the skills and qualities you admire.

When approaching a potential mentor, be clear about why you are seeking their guidance and what you hope to achieve through the mentorship. Articulate your career goals and how their experience aligns with these objectives. It's important to express your commitment to the mentorship process and how you plan to contribute to a mutually beneficial relationship.

Seeking feedback and advice from mentors is an ongoing process that requires openness and receptivity. Feedback from a mentor can provide new perspectives on tackling challenges and seizing opportunities. It's important to approach feedback sessions with an open mind, ready to listen and reflect on the insights provided. Constructive criticism, when taken positively, can significantly improve leadership capabilities and self-assurance. Mentorship is not just about receiving guidance; it is also about active learning. Take the initiative to apply the insights gained from your mentor in your day-to-day work. Reflect on what worked well and what didn't, and discuss these reflections in subsequent meetings. This iterative learning process helps in refining your skills and enhancing your leadership effectiveness. Creating an action plan based on mentor feedback is a practical approach to implementing the lessons learned. Set achievable goals, outline the steps needed to reach them, and regularly review your progress with your mentor. This structured approach ensures that the mentorship is goal-oriented and results-driven, contributing significantly to your confidence and leadership development.

Moreover, mentors can play a critical role in expanding your professional network. Through their connections, you can gain access to new opportunities, resources, and support systems. Having a broader network can enhance your influence and visibility within your industry. Cultivating these relationships can lead to collaborative projects, partnerships, and even potential career advancements.

Acknowledge Accomplishments

Acknowledging progress involves more than just giving yourself a pat on the back. It means genuinely celebrating incremental successes and milestones, no matter how small they may seem. These acknowledgments serve as tangible evidence of your journey and achievements. For instance, completing a successful presentation or negotiating a beneficial deal are such milestones.

Each step forward, even if it's not a major leap, contributes to building your confidence bit by bit. This practice not only helps in recognizing your growth but also in reinforcing the belief that you are capable and competent.

Creating a culture of recognition and appreciation within both individual and team frameworks plays a significant role in fostering confidence. As a leader, it is important to acknowledge not only your own achievements but also those of your team members. When team efforts are recognized, it builds collective morale and shows everyone that their contributions matter.

Simple acts such as verbal appreciation during team meetings, written accolades in company newsletters, or even small celebratory events can significantly boost self-esteem. This culture of mutual appreciation makes everyone feel valued and acknowledged, reducing feelings of inadequacy and boosting overall confidence.

Reflecting on accomplishments is a fundamental practice in building self-esteem. Taking time to look back on what you have achieved helps in internalizing these successes and viewing them as a testament to your capabilities. For example, at the end of each week or month, dedicate some time to reflect on what went well, what you accomplished, and how you've grown. This reflection not only keeps your achievements at the forefront of your mind but also provides motivation for future endeavors. Documenting these reflections can be particularly helpful. Keeping a journal where you jot down your successes and how you feel about them can serve as an uplifting reminder of your journey whenever self-doubt creeps in.

Leveraging past successes as motivation to tackle future goals with resilience is a powerful strategy. The knowledge that you have succeeded in the past provides a strong foundation upon which to build future success. When faced with new challenges, recalling previous victories can instill confidence and reassure you of your abilities. If you successfully led a challenging project before, use that experience as a benchmark the next time you face a difficult task. Remind yourself of the skills and strategies you employed and consider how they can be adapted to current challenges. This approach nurtures a resilient mindset, making you more adept at handling new obstacles with confidence.

Moreover, fostering a mindset that values progress over perfection is crucial. It is common to fall into the trap of all-or-nothing thinking, where anything less than perfect is deemed a failure. However, focusing on progress acknowledges that improvement is a continuous process. Celebrate the fact that you are moving forward, regardless of the pace or magnitude of the steps taken. This shift in perspective helps in alleviating the pressure to be flawless and instead encourages a healthy appreciation for steady growth and effort. It's also beneficial to surround yourself with a supportive network that recognizes and celebrates your achievements.

Engage with mentors, colleagues, and friends who offer genuine encouragement and constructive feedback. Their positive reinforcement can act as an external validation that complements your internal acknowledgment of achievements. When others celebrate your successes, it reaffirms your efforts and contribution, providing an additional boost to your self-esteem.

Final Thoughts

This chapter has explored various strategies to help women leaders build confidence and overcome self-doubt. From recognizing and addressing imposter syndrome to developing a growth mindset, these techniques are designed to empower you in your leadership journey. Building a strong support system, setting achievable goals, and practicing self-compassion are all crucial steps toward fostering self-belief and resilience. Additionally, engaging in regular reflection and mindfulness practices can provide clarity and reduce anxiety, further enhancing confidence.

Ultimately, the goal is to create a supportive environment where women leaders can thrive. By educating oneself about imposter syndrome and advocating for an open workplace culture, you can break free from self-limiting beliefs and embrace your full potential. Celebrating small wins and seeking mentorship are also pivotal in reinforcing self-worth and motivation.

Through these collective efforts, you can navigate your career with greater assurance and lead with confidence, inspiring others along the way. In the next chapter, we're going to look at what unique strengths female leaders bring to the table. We'll learn how our emotional intelligence, empathy, communication skills, and resilience all contribute to our success as leaders. When you're aware of these inherent traits, you'll be able to navigate obstacles more effectively and will achieve the success you're aiming for.

Chapter 3:
Leveraging Unique Leadership Qualities

Being different is critical. –Ana Patricia Botín

Ana Patricia Botín, Executive Chair of Banco Santander explained of her drive for new initiatives: "Being different is critical." Female leaders bring distinct strengths to the table, such as emotional intelligence, empathy, effective communication, and resilience. These qualities not only enhance their leadership capabilities but also contribute to creating more dynamic and inclusive work environments.

This chapter delves into the core aspects of what makes female leadership uniquely impactful. It begins by exploring the importance of recognizing and embracing distinctive traits like emotional intelligence, highlighting how self-awareness and empathy play vital roles in leadership. You'll then journey through practical strategies for managing conflicts and maintaining composure under pressure, followed by insights on leveraging emotions as strengths. The chapter concludes by examining the resilience and adaptability that many women possess, offering actionable advice on how to cultivate these qualities for personal and team growth. Through these discussions, aspiring female leaders such as yourself will find valuable guidance to develop their skills and lead with confidence.

Identifying Unique Traits

Understanding and embracing the distinctive qualities that women bring to leadership roles is essential in creating a more dynamic and inclusive work environment.

Women leaders often excel in emotional intelligence, leveraging emotions as a strength, managing conflicts effectively, and demonstrating remarkable resilience and adaptability. Recognizing these qualities not only empowers female leaders but also enhances the overall effectiveness of their teams and organizations.

One of the most significant strengths that women bring to leadership is their high level of emotional intelligence. Emotional intelligence (EQ) encompasses self-awareness, empathy, and the ability to navigate interpersonal dynamics effectively. Developing self-awareness allows female leaders to understand their own emotions, which can influence their decision-making processes and interactions with others. By being aware of your emotions, you can regulate your responses, maintaining composure in high-pressure situations.

Empathy, a core component of EQ, enables female leaders to connect with their team members on a deeper level. Understanding and appreciating the emotions and perspectives of others fosters an environment of trust and collaboration. As an empathetic leader, you can better support your teams, address their concerns, and provide guidance tailored to individual needs. This approach not only enhances team morale but also drives collective success by fostering a sense of belonging and mutual respect.

Navigating interpersonal dynamics is another area where female leaders often shine. Effective communication is crucial in any leadership role, and women tend to excel in this aspect. We possess strong verbal and non-verbal communication skills, ensuring that our vision and goals are clearly conveyed to the teams we lead. Transparent communication builds trust and reduces misunderstandings, laying a solid foundation for a high-functioning team. Additionally, women are better listeners. Our active listening skills help us gather valuable insights from our team members, promoting a culture of open dialogue and continuous improvement.

Leveraging emotions as a strength in decision-making and communication is another distinctive quality that women bring to leadership. Emotions play a vital role in human interactions, and female leaders often use their emotional awareness to build effective connections.

For instance, when making decisions, women consider not only the logical aspects but also the emotional impact on their team members. This holistic approach ensures that decisions are well-rounded and considerate of everyone's well-being.

In communication, women leaders harness their emotional intelligence to convey messages with compassion and clarity. By acknowledging and addressing the emotions of their audience, they create a supportive environment where team members feel valued and understood. This emotional resonance helps in building strong relationships, enhancing team cohesion, and driving collective success.

Managing conflicts by recognizing and regulating emotions is another area where female leaders excel. Conflicts are inevitable in any organization, and how they are managed can significantly impact team dynamics. Women leaders utilize their emotional intelligence to identify the root causes of conflicts and address them effectively. By recognizing the emotions involved, you can approach conflict resolution with empathy and understanding, leading to more constructive outcomes.

Regulating your own emotions during conflict is equally important. Female leaders who maintain their composure and respond calmly to challenging situations set a positive example for their teams. This approach diffuses tension and encourages a problem-solving mindset.

By fostering an environment where conflicts are resolved amicably, you can contribute to a healthier and more productive workplace.

Resilience and adaptability are also hallmark qualities of female leaders. Throughout history, women have demonstrated remarkable resilience in the face of adversity. This innate ability to bounce back from setbacks and view challenges as opportunities for growth positions women leaders to guide their teams through uncertain times effectively. Resilience is not just about enduring difficulties; it's about learning from them and emerging stronger.

Adaptability is closely linked to resilience. In rapidly changing environments, the ability to pivot and adjust strategies is crucial. Female leaders often excel in this regard, swiftly adapting to new circumstances and inspiring their teams to do the same.

When you're willing to embrace change and turn obstacles into opportunities, you foster a culture of innovation and continuous improvement. On top of that, women often have less ego than others, making it easier for us to excel. Moreover, resilient and adaptable leaders create a sense of stability within their teams. When faced with challenges, a confident and positive demeanor reassures team members, boosting their confidence and motivation. By viewing setbacks as temporary and surmountable, women leaders instill a growth mindset in their teams, encouraging them to persevere and strive for excellence.

Embracing these distinctive qualities not only benefits female leaders but also enhances the overall effectiveness of organizations. As mentioned before, diverse leadership teams, including those with strong female representation, lead to better decision-making and improved business performance. Women's unique strengths contribute to a more inclusive and empathetic workplace, where diverse perspectives are valued and leveraged for success.

Enhancing Emotional Intelligence

Strengthening emotional awareness and empathy is a critical step toward enhancing leadership effectiveness. Embracing these qualities allows female leaders to foster a more inclusive, supportive, and productive work environment. In this section, you'll find practical guidance on how to cultivate empathy, self-reflection, and awareness, practice active listening, create supportive environments, and recognize biases.

Self-Reflection and Awareness

Cultivating mindfulness and understanding personal triggers to manage emotions effectively is foundational for any leader. Self-reflection begins with taking time each day to introspect on one's thoughts and feelings. Journaling can be a powerful tool here. By writing down your emotions, you can identify patterns and understand what situations trigger certain responses. This process of continuous self-awareness is crucial in managing stress and making rational decisions under pressure. Being mindful means being present at the moment and fully engaged with your surroundings and the people you interact with. It involves paying attention to your inner state without judgment, which helps in recognizing your emotions before they influence your behavior. One effective way to cultivate mindfulness is through meditation and breathing exercises. These practices enhance your ability to stay calm and focused, especially in high-stress situations, allowing you to respond rather than react impulsively.

> **Success Strategy**: Not everyone can name their emotions, especially the more difficult emotions. Create an emotion wheel to expand your emotional vocabulary and identify how you're feeling more accurately. It will also help if you explore how different emotions can manifest in your daily life.

Active Listening

Another essential aspect is active listening. Leaders often need to wear multiple hats—mentors, coaches, mediators—and active listening lies at the heart of all these roles. Active listening goes beyond just hearing words; it involves engaging with the speaker, asking clarifying questions, and paraphrasing to ensure understanding. This not only demonstrates empathy but also builds trust and rapport with team members.

Practicing active listening requires putting away distractions, such as mobile phones or computers, and giving the speaker your full attention. Non-verbal cues like nodding and maintaining eye contact show that you are genuinely interested in their perspective. Remember, the goal is to understand, not to reply immediately. Reflecting on what they've said and providing feedback that shows you value their input can significantly strengthen workplace relationships.

> **Success Strategy**: A big part of active listening is providing feedback to the speaker during conversations. Nodding, saying "Yes," or repeating what the person said back to them to make sure that you're understanding them correctly will improve your active listening skills. It will also make them feel validated and can help clarify their message to avoid misunderstandings.

Creating a Supportive and Inclusive Environment

Empathetic leadership is about creating an environment where every team member feels valued and supported. This involves recognizing and addressing the unique needs and challenges faced by each individual. For instance, ensuring that everyone has the resources they need to succeed, from professional development opportunities to flexible working arrangements, can go a long way in fostering a positive workplace culture. An inclusive environment encourages open communication and collaboration. Leaders should actively seek out and include diverse perspectives when making decisions. This not only enriches the decision-making process but also signals to team members that their voices matter. Facilitating regular team-building activities and having open-door policies can also promote inclusivity and camaraderie, making employees feel more connected and engaged.

> **Success Strategy**: Recognizing and rewarding team achievements will boost morale and keep your team motivated. Moreover, it will create a supportive environment aimed at growing together.

Recognizing and Managing Biases

A leader's ability to recognize and manage their biases is crucial in making fair and unbiased decisions. Everyone has unconscious biases that can affect their judgment and actions. Being aware of these biases and actively working to counteract them is essential for equitable leadership. One effective strategy is undergoing a 360-degree assessment, which includes feedback from peers, subordinates, and supervisors. This can highlight any blind spots and provide insights into areas where biases might exist. Additionally, seeking continuous education and training on diversity and inclusion can help you better understand and appreciate different perspectives. Implementing structured decision-making processes, such as using standardized criteria for hiring or promotions, can also mitigate the influence of personal biases. By committing to transparency and fairness, leaders can build a culture of trust and respect within their teams.

> **Success Strategy**: Do research on successful female leaders who have navigated bias in their careers. This will motivate you during times when you feel deflated.

How High Emotional Intelligence (EQ) Can Propel Your Career

The job market is highly competitive, especially if you're a woman. Your technical skills and knowledge alone won't cut it; however, EQ has become a critical differentiator between those who get the job and those who don't. Here's how it can benefit your professional journey:

1. **Enhanced Communication and Collaboration**

    - People with high EQ are great at active listening, clear and concise communication, and adapting their communication style to different audiences. This fosters strong relationships, builds trust, and enables effective collaboration.

    - They navigate conflict constructively, seeking to understand different perspectives and find mutually beneficial solutions. This minimizes misunderstandings and fosters a positive and productive work environment.

    - By understanding and managing their own emotions and those of others, high EQ individuals inspire and motivate their team members, fostering a collaborative and supportive environment.

2. **Improved Decision-Making and Problem-Solving**

    - They recognize how their emotions influence their decisions and take steps to manage them effectively. This leads to more rational and objective decision-making, reducing impulsive choices and improving problem-solving abilities.

    - Individuals with high EQ effectively manage stress, maintaining composure under pressure and adapting to challenging situations. This allows them to think clearly, make sound decisions, and navigate complex situations effectively.

    - They have the ability to bounce back from setbacks and learn from their mistakes. This resilience allows them to persevere through challenges and maintain a positive outlook, crucial for long-term career success.

3. **Increased Self-Awareness and Personal Growth**

    - High EQ individuals have a clear understanding of their strengths and weaknesses, allowing them to leverage their talents and address areas for improvement. This self-awareness fosters continuous learning and personal growth.

    - They can readily adapt to changing circumstances and embrace new challenges. This flexibility allows them to thrive in dynamic environments and seize new opportunities.

    - By understanding their values and motivations, they make career choices that align with their passions and aspirations. This leads to greater job satisfaction, fulfillment, and a sense of purpose in their work.

4. Enhanced Career Advancement and Leadership Potential

- They're able to build strong relationships with colleagues, clients, and superiors. This fosters trust, respect, and collaboration, leading to increased visibility and opportunities for advancement.

- Individuals with high EQ inspire and motivate their teams, creating a positive and productive work environment. This leadership potential makes them valuable assets to any organization and increases their chances of promotion.

- They navigate career transitions and challenges effectively, maintaining a positive attitude and adapting to new situations. This resilience enhances their long-term career prospects and increases their ability to thrive in a changing job market.

In conclusion, you're an asset to any organization because as a woman, you already possess a higher EQ than men. By developing your emotional intelligence even further, you can enhance your communication, decision-making, and leadership skills, ultimately propelling your career toward success and fulfillment.

Utilizing Empathy in Leadership

Harnessing empathy as a powerful leadership tool is vital for female leaders aiming to connect with their team members and drive success. Empathy allows leaders to understand and resonate with the feelings of others, which can significantly impact decision-making, team dynamics, and overall organizational culture. One essential aspect of empathetic leadership is making informed decisions that consider the well-being of stakeholders while balancing objective-driven strategies. Leaders who practice empathy are better equipped to recognize the signs of overwork among employees, potentially preventing burnout before it becomes an issue.

This proactive approach ensures that team members remain engaged and productive. For instance, taking a few extra minutes each week to check in with team members can reveal how they manage their workload and whether they need support. By integrating empathy into decision-making processes, leaders can create a more sustainable and humane work environment (Center for Creative Leadership, 2023).

Inclusive decision-making is another vital component of empathetic leadership. Valuing diverse perspectives within teams fosters innovation and creativity, as different viewpoints can lead to more comprehensive solutions. Empathetic leaders actively seek input from all team members, ensuring that everyone feels heard and valued. This inclusivity not only enhances decision-making but also promotes a sense of belonging among team members. When leaders demonstrate that they value diverse opinions, team members are more likely to contribute their unique insights, leading to richer discussions and better outcomes.

Moreover, promoting a culture of feedback and learning from failures without fear of retribution is integral to empathetic leadership. By fostering a safe space for feedback, you enable team members to learn from your experiences and improve continuously. This culture of openness and learning not only enhances individual performance but also strengthens the team's resilience and adaptability. When team members know that their leader will support them through setbacks, they are more likely to take calculated risks and innovate, driving the organization forward.

Empathetic leadership also involves recognizing personal struggles and offering support when needed. The lines between work and personal life are increasingly blurred, and empathetic leaders acknowledge that their team members are individuals with complex lives. Demonstrating compassion when team members face personal challenges can strengthen bonds and foster loyalty. For instance, showing understanding and providing flexibility during difficult times can significantly impact an individual's well-being and performance. This level of care and consideration builds a strong foundation of trust and mutual respect within the team. Finally, cultivating empathy requires consistent effort and reflection. You should regularly reflect on your interactions and consider how you can improve your empathetic responses. Engaging in self-reflection will help you become more aware of your own biases and emotional triggers, enabling you to manage your reactions more effectively. This practice also enhances emotional intelligence, allowing you to navigate interpersonal dynamics with greater sensitivity and understanding.

Final Insights

Embracing and harnessing your inherent strengths as a female leader can transform not only your leadership journey but also the dynamic of your team. By recognizing and developing emotional intelligence, you become more self-aware, empathetic, and excellent at navigating interpersonal dynamics. These qualities allow you to manage conflicts with grace, make well-rounded decisions, and communicate effectively. Your ability to leverage emotions as strengths fosters a supportive and inclusive environment where team members feel valued and understood.

Moreover, resilience and adaptability are key traits that underpin successful leadership. Facing challenges with confidence and turning obstacles into opportunities for growth sets a positive example and encourages a culture of innovation. As you continue to embrace these distinctive qualities and promote inclusivity within your organization, you'll help drive better decision-making and overall success. This chapter underscores the importance of knowing and utilizing your unique strengths, reinforcing the impact women leaders have in creating more effective, diverse, and empathetic workplaces.

In Chapter 4, we're going to look at the role having a support network plays in your career success. I always thought that networking was handing my business card to someone else—there, I networked. How wrong I was! After reading the next chapter, I hope you realize the value forming long-term connections has on your career.

Chapter 4:

Networking and Building Supportive Relationships

Never doubt that a small group of thoughtful committed citizens can change the world. Indeed, it is the only thing that ever has. –Margaret Mead

Cultivating a solid network can open doors to mentorship, knowledge sharing, and increased visibility within and outside your industry and in your life. Networking is more than just exchanging business cards; it's about forming meaningful connections that can lead to long-term professional support and collaboration.

In this chapter, we will delve into the significance of networking and how it plays a crucial role in career development, particularly for women aspiring to leadership roles or looking to grow their businesses. We'll explore various strategies for effective networking, such as attending industry conferences, leveraging social media, and setting clear networking objectives. Additionally, we'll discuss the importance of building a diverse network to gain different perspectives and resources. By understanding and applying these concepts, you'll be empowered to create a supportive network that fosters both personal and professional growth.

Importance of Networking

Throughout my entire career, I have only interviewed and gotten a job outside of my network once. Networking is a cornerstone for leadership success and can significantly impact your career growth, particularly for women aspiring to leadership positions or looking to develop their businesses.

Understanding why networking is so crucial and how it can be leveraged effectively is essential. Building connections is one of the most important aspects of networking. Establishing relationships can open doors to opportunities that might otherwise remain closed. For instance, attending industry conferences and seminars allows you to meet like-minded individuals who may offer insights into new trends and innovations within your field. These interactions not only broaden your horizons but also provide valuable mentorship opportunities. By sharing experiences and knowledge, established leaders can guide you through challenging situations, helping you avoid common pitfalls women face and leveraging their experience to support your growth.

I went to a Women's Leadership conference in San Francisco and met many executive women. While I was there, I received a job offer from a company with a questionable culture and a revolving door of leaders into the position I was being offered. The women, whom I had just met, helped me negotiate and ultimately win the job—protecting myself if there was an issue with the culture or company. I still keep in touch with a few of these women today.

Networking also facilitates access to a broader range of resources and knowledge. Engaging with a diverse network means tapping into various expertise and perspectives that can enhance your problem-solving capabilities. This is particularly beneficial in corporate settings where collaboration across departments is often necessary. Women in leadership roles can benefit greatly from this exchange of ideas, as it enables them to bring innovative solutions to the table, thereby increasing their value within the organization. A well-rounded network acts as a repository of information and support, providing different viewpoints that enrich decision-making processes.

Professional growth is another significant advantage of effective networking. Building a robust professional network can directly lead to career advancement and personal development. According to Stobierski (2019), many business leaders use their networks to identify career opportunities before they become public knowledge. This early awareness gives them a competitive edge. In most of the jobs I have had,

I was spoken to about the role before the position was advertised. In many cases, the job was created specifically for me because I brought unique skills to the table.

For women aiming for leadership roles, this can mean the difference between stagnation and rapid career progression. Furthermore, networking can facilitate introductions to key decision-makers who can champion your cause within the company or industry, enhancing your visibility and credibility.

Networking is not just about forming superficial connections but developing meaningful relationships that require ongoing effort and nurturing. Regularly engaging with your network, whether through coffee meetings, virtual catch-ups, or industry events, helps maintain and strengthen these bonds. Over time, these relationships become mutually beneficial, with each party investing in and supporting the other's success.

Effective Networking Strategies

In today's increasingly interconnected world, the ability to network strategically and build supportive relationships is a vital skill. Networking can open doors to new opportunities for women aspiring to leadership positions, offer valuable insights, and help in career advancement. This section provides practical strategies to help you effectively navigate the networking landscape.

Another way to networks is intentionally seeking out connections that align with your career goals. It starts by identifying the key individuals or groups in your field who can provide guidance, support, and opportunities. For example, if you're aiming for a leadership role in the tech industry, connecting with female leaders already excelling in that field can be invaluable. Make a list of people you want to meet and prepare to approach them with specific questions related to your professional interests. Then, attend industry-specific events, such as conferences and seminars, where these influential figures are likely to be present.

Setting networking objectives is another crucial component. Before attending any networking event or reaching out to potential contacts, set clear and achievable goals.

Do you want to learn about career progression within a particular company? Are you looking to gain insights into the latest industry trends? By setting these objectives, you create purposeful interactions that are more likely to result in beneficial outcomes. A good practice is to formulate what you hope to achieve from each meeting or event. For instance, aim to leave each interaction with at least one actionable piece of advice or a new connection.

Leveraging social media and professional platforms has become an indispensable tool in modern networking. Platforms like LinkedIn, Twitter, and even industry-specific forums allow you to connect with professionals around the globe. Start by optimizing your profiles on these platforms to reflect your current skills, experiences, and career aspirations. Engaging actively by posting relevant content, participating in discussions, and sharing expert opinions can significantly enhance your visibility and credibility. Remember to maintain a professional image online, as prospective employers and collaborators often scout social media profiles to gauge suitability.

> **Success Strategy**: You should maintain a genuine presence that reflects your personal values while avoiding an over-polished persona on your social media. Always maintain a respectful tone and steer clear of controversial or divisive issues.

Once initial contact is made, focus on active listening. Asking open-ended questions and genuinely responding to people's answers fosters meaningful conversations. People appreciate when their experiences and opinions are valued, making them more willing to extend support or share information. Follow up after meetings with personalized messages to reaffirm your interest and appreciation. This could be a quick email thanking them for their time and mentioning something specific you discussed. Keeping in touch periodically helps in nurturing these relationships over the long term.

Another powerful strategy is engaging in targeted online communities. While broad networks like LinkedIn are beneficial, niche communities often provide deeper, more focused interactions. Join forums, groups, or associations related to your industry or interests. Consistently contribute by answering queries, sharing resources, and offering support. Over time, this builds your reputation as a knowledgeable and helpful figure, fostering authentic relationships that can translate into real-world opportunities. Strategic generosity is another compelling networking tactic. Offer value to others without expecting immediate returns. Share industry insights, introduce valuable contacts, or provide feedback on projects. This not only establishes you as a resourceful and genuine professional but also strengthens trust-based relationships. In turn, people are more likely to reciprocate, creating a cycle of mutual support and benefit.

Adopting a help-first networking philosophy emphasizes prioritizing others' needs. When interacting, focus on how you can assist them rather than immediately seeking your benefit. This approach fosters goodwill and builds stronger, more lasting connections. Ask, "How can I help you today?" and listen attentively to their responses. Empathy and understanding can position you as a trusted ally, making others more inclined to support you in return.

Building Alliances

By engaging in strategic partnerships, you can leverage collective strengths and resources, enhancing your ability to navigate challenges and accomplish objectives.

Strategic Partnerships

Forming alliances with like-minded individuals or organizations is a fundamental step toward building a supportive network. These partnerships are formed based on shared values, goals, and interests, creating a foundation of mutual trust and respect. For instance, a female entrepreneur might partner with another business owner who shares her vision for sustainable practices in their industry. This alliance allows them to pool their expertise, resources, and networks, amplifying their influence and reach within their market. When forming strategic partnerships, it is crucial to identify potential partners whose goals align with your own and to establish clear objectives and expectations for the collaboration. Collaborating with others can significantly amplify one's influence and impact. When women come together to work toward common goals, they not only share the workload but also bring diverse perspectives and skills to the table. For example, a group of female leaders in the tech industry might collaborate on a project that aims to increase diversity and inclusion within their companies. By combining their efforts, they are more likely to create meaningful change and inspire others to join their cause.

Alliances offer collective strength and shared resources for common objectives. Collective strength comes from the combined abilities and assets of all members involved in an alliance. This means that each member can benefit from the resources that others bring to the table, whether it's knowledge, funding, or access to networks. An illustration of this is seen in advocacy groups. When multiple organizations with similar missions band together, they can present a united front that is harder for policymakers to ignore.

> ## Jessica's Story
>
> As a woman working in the finance industry, I've often felt isolated and like I was navigating challenges alone. The industry can be male-dominated, and it can be difficult to find mentors or peers who truly understand the unique obstacles women face. A few years ago, I decided to be proactive about changing that.
>
> I reached out to a few female colleagues in similar roles. At first, I was nervous; would they see me as a threat or be unwilling to collaborate? But to my surprise, they were incredibly receptive and eager to connect. We started meeting regularly, both in person and virtually, to share challenges, brainstorm solutions, and learn from each other.
>
> One of the biggest benefits has been simply having a supportive network of women who "get it." We're able to vent about frustrating meetings, celebrate wins, and offer advice and encouragement. It's made the day-to-day grind so much more manageable, knowing I have this group of women in my corner. But the partnership has also brought tangible benefits to our work. By combining our diverse skillsets and perspectives, we've been able to tackle projects more efficiently and creatively. One of us might have expertise in financial modeling, while another excels at client relationships. We divvy up tasks based on our strengths, ensuring a higher quality end product. We've also used our partnership to advocate for change within our organizations. As a unified front, we've been able to push for things like more equitable parental leave policies, unconscious bias training, and increased representation of women in leadership. Our collective voice carries so much more weight.
>
> Overall, forming this strategic partnership with other women in my industry has been one of the most rewarding and productive decisions I've made in my career. It's reduced my workload, expanded my capabilities, and given me a powerful support system. I'd encourage any woman feeling isolated in a male-dominated field to seek out similar connections. The benefits are immeasurable.

Mentorship and Sponsorship

Mentorship involves cultivating relationships with experienced mentors who provide valuable guidance and advice. Experienced mentors can offer a wealth of insights drawn from their own careers, which can be instrumental for mentees navigating challenges in their professional journeys. For instance, a mentor's feedback on handling complex projects or interpersonal conflicts at work can significantly impact how these situations are managed effectively.

One of the most beneficial aspects of mentorship is the opportunity it presents for skill development and knowledge transfer. Through regular interactions and discussions, mentees can learn new skills, gain confidence, and broaden their perspectives. A mentor might share techniques for effective public speaking, strategies for managing time efficiently, or tips for leading a diverse team. These skills are not only essential for immediate job performance but also critical for long-term career development. Mentorship relationships can also provide emotional support, acting as a safe space where mentees can express concerns, seek validation, and gain encouragement. This supportive environment can be especially beneficial for women facing unique workplace challenges, such as gender bias or balancing work-life demands. The reassurance and motivation from a mentor can help build resilience and self-assurance, empowering mentees to pursue ambitious goals.

> **Success Strategy**: Always assess a possible mentor's level of experience and relevance in your field. You should also look out for red flags in mentor behavior, such as lack of support or competitiveness. Establish boundaries and always do your best to maintain a healthy mentor-mentee relationship.

Sponsorship, on the other hand, goes beyond mentorship by actively advocating and championing others for career opportunities. Sponsors leverage their influence within an organization to promote their protégés, providing access to high-visibility projects, key decision-makers, and critical career opportunities that would otherwise be out of reach. Unlike mentors, who primarily offer advice and support, sponsors use their power and networks to open doors and create tangible career advancements for their protégés. A significant benefit of having a sponsor is increased visibility within the organization.

Sponsors ensure that their protégés are noticed by senior leaders and considered for important assignments. For example, a sponsor might recommend a protégé for a major cross-departmental project, nominate them for a leadership training program, or advocate for their promotion. This level of support can be transformative, accelerating career growth and enhancing leadership prospects.

Moreover, sponsors often challenge their protégés with stretch assignments—tasks that are more demanding than their usual responsibilities. These challenging assignments help protégés develop new skills, demonstrate their capabilities, and gain experience in unfamiliar areas. Such opportunities not only prepare protégés for higher-level roles but also signal their potential to the broader organization. The impact of mentorship and sponsorship on career development can be significant. According to research, individuals with mentors are more likely to report having opportunities to learn and grow at work, feel more engaged, and have a clearer plan for their career development (Inc, 2023). Similarly, employees with sponsors are more likely to receive promotions, experience greater job satisfaction, and earn higher salaries compared to those without sponsors (Page Personnel, n.d.).

Final Thoughts

Networking is an indispensable tool for women aiming to enhance their leadership capabilities. This chapter highlighted how cultivating professional networks and supportive relationships opens doors to new opportunities, provides valuable mentorship, and facilitates access to diverse resources. By engaging with a broad range of professionals, women can tap into different expertise and perspectives, which enrich problem-solving skills and foster innovative solutions. Building strong connections based on trust and mutual respect not only offers emotional and professional support during challenging times but also creates paths for career advancement and personal growth.

Effective networking goes beyond just forming connections; it involves nurturing meaningful relationships through continuous engagement. Regular interactions, whether in person or online, help maintain these bonds, leading to mutually beneficial outcomes.

The next chapter is an important one. We'll be looking at something many of us have experienced or are likely to experience at one point or another: gender bias and stereotyping. The ability to recognize these ingrained prejudices is the first step toward addressing them. So, let's arm you with some strategies for overcoming this unfortunate part of being a woman with a career.

Chapter 5:
Navigating Gender Bias and Stereotypes

The way to overcome people's biases is typically by delivering results. No one can really refute the results you deliver. –Lisa Borders

Gender biases, both explicit and implicit, often shape our perceptions and actions subconsciously, impacting decision-making and creating barriers to equality. Recognizing these ingrained prejudices is a critical step toward addressing them. Implicit biases, which operate below the level of conscious awareness, silently influence our views on gender roles, leading to unfair assumptions about capabilities based on gender.

By bringing these hidden biases to light, individuals and organizations can begin to dismantle them, paving the way for more equitable treatment of all employees.

This chapter delves into various strategies for overcoming gender bias and stereotypes in the corporate world. We will cover actionable steps to counteract these biases in decision-making processes, such as ensuring objective criteria for hiring and promotions.

Additionally, there I share how to challenge damaging stereotypes that may hinder your leadership opportunities by highlighting successful female leaders and emphasizing the importance of fostering supportive mentorship programs.

Furthermore, the chapter emphasizes the importance of creating a culture of awareness through diversity training, inclusive language practices, and continuous education, thereby nurturing an environment where every individual feels valued and respected regardless of their gender.

Recognizing Biases

Recognizing gender biases in the workplace is a crucial step toward creating an environment that allows everyone to thrive equally. It is often challenging to address something we might not even realize exists, such as implicit bias. Implicit or unconscious biases are deeply ingrained stereotypes that unknowingly influence our perceptions and actions. By identifying these subconscious biases, we open the door to challenging and changing them.

Understanding Implicit Bias

Implicit bias refers to the unconscious attitudes or stereotypes that we hold about certain groups of people. For example, throughout my life, I've had people ask me what I do. When I told them, they always wanted to know what I did with my kids during the day. Of course, my husband never got asked this question. What's more, it always felt as if telling them I do the same with my kids as they do—send them to school—wasn't good enough of an answer for them. These biases can influence our behavior and decisions without us even realizing it.

Biases are not necessarily reflective of our intent, but they can have significant impacts on our interactions and judgments. Recognizing and addressing implicit bias is essential for promoting fairness and equality in various aspects of life, including workplaces, educational settings, and societal interactions.

Why Understanding Implicit Bias Matters

Understanding implicit bias is crucial because it directly impacts our interactions with others. For instance, in hiring practices, implicit bias can lead to favoritism toward certain candidates based on stereotypes. A manager may unconsciously prefer candidates with similar backgrounds and experiences, which can limit diversity within the team. This lack of diverse perspectives can impede creativity and problem-solving, making it vital for organizations to recognize and mitigate these biases. Identifying implicit biases often involves self-reflection and awareness of one's own thoughts and behaviors. Engaging in open conversations about diversity can help reveal biases.

Participating in assessments or implicit bias tests can provide insights into unconscious preferences. Observing reactions in different situations can highlight areas where biases may exist. Keeping a journal can aid in recognizing patterns in thinking or behavior that may indicate bias.

Taking Action Against Implicit Bias

Educating yourself about different cultures, communities, and experiences can help challenge existing biases. Reading books, attending workshops, or participating in group discussions about diversity and inclusion can provide valuable perspectives. Continuous learning is essential for fostering understanding and empathy.

Engaging With Diverse Groups

Actively engaging with individuals from diverse backgrounds can also help to counter implicit biases. By interacting with people who have different experiences, you can gain insights that challenge preconceived notions. This might include joining clubs, attending cultural events, or volunteering in diverse communities.

Practicing Mindfulness

Mindfulness practices can also be instrumental in addressing implicit biases. Being aware of your thoughts and reactions in various situations allows you to recognize biased responses when they occur.

Techniques such as meditation or journaling can enhance your awareness and enable you to reflect on your biases more deeply.

Developing Structured Decision-Making Processes

Creating structured decision-making processes can reduce the impact of implicit biases in professional settings. For instance, using standardized evaluation criteria in hiring can help ensure that all candidates are assessed based on the same factors rather than subjective opinions. Incorporating diverse panels in recruitment or organizational decisions can also mitigate individual biases and promote a more equitable atmosphere.

Monitoring Progress

Acknowledging the existence of such biases is the first step to mitigating their influence. Once you become aware of your biases, it's possible to consciously counteract them in decision-making processes. For instance, ensuring that hiring and promotion criteria are based on objective measures rather than subjective judgments can help minimize the impact of these biases. Encouraging open discussions about bias within teams also plays a significant role, fostering an atmosphere where questioning and learning from one another becomes the norm.

The detrimental effects of stereotyping cannot be overstated, particularly when it comes to women's leadership opportunities. Stereotypes paint a narrow picture of what individuals from different genders can achieve and how they should behave. For instance, women might be stereotyped as being less assertive or less capable of handling high-stress situations. Such stereotypes can significantly hinder women from being considered for leadership roles, impacting their career growth and the overall diversity within leadership teams.

To combat these stereotypes, demonstrating your skill through consistent performance and success in the corporate environment goes a long way. It's also good to communicate your ideas and contributions in meetings to ensure your voices are heard. Ultimately, you need to show the world that you're there and that you're doing a stellar job, so take the initiative to seek feedback and engage in self-advocacy. This will enhance your visibility and presence. Moreover, encouraging inclusive language and behavior is essential.

Simple practices, such as using gender-neutral terms in job descriptions and during evaluations, can significantly reduce implicit bias. Regularly reviewing policies and procedures to ensure they don't favor one gender over another is also vital. Leaders within organizations need to create an environment where everyone feels seen, heard, and valued, regardless of their gender.

Advocacy Strategies

In the face of gender biases and stereotypes, advocating for yourself is essential. This section provides tools and techniques to help you navigate these challenges effectively, focusing on key areas like self-promotion, building allies, negotiation skills, and assertiveness training.

- Let's delve into self-promotion, a critical skill for countering gender bias. Women often struggle with promoting their achievements due to societal norms that expect humility. However, confidently presenting your accomplishments can help shift perceptions and open doors. Start by keeping track of your successes, no matter how small they seem. Document your achievements and be ready to share them during performance reviews or casual conversations. Practice talking about your work in a way that highlights your contributions without seeming boastful. For example, instead of saying, "I led the project," you could say, "Our team achieved significant milestones under my guidance." This not only showcases your leadership but also emphasizes the collective effort.

- As discussed in Chapter 4, building allies within your organization is another powerful strategy. Forming alliances helps create a support network that amplifies your voice and provides mutual backing. Begin by identifying colleagues who share similar goals and values. Engage with them through informal meetings, lunches, or collaborative projects. Express your willingness to support their initiatives and ask for their support in return. Mentors and sponsors can also provide guidance and advocate for your advancement.

- Negotiation skills are crucial for navigating biased situations, especially when it comes to salary and promotions. Women often hesitate to negotiate, fearing backlash or being perceived as aggressive, yet negotiating is vital for ensuring fair treatment. Start by researching industry standards and prepare a solid case for your requests, backed by data and evidence of your performance. During negotiations, focus on the value you bring to the organization rather than comparing yourself to others. Practice active listening and respond thoughtfully to objections. If faced with resistance, stay calm and reiterate your points clearly and confidently. Remember, negotiation is a dialogue, not a confrontation. Building this skill over time will enhance your ability to advocate for yourself effectively.

- Assertiveness training is another essential tool for challenging stereotypes and biases constructively. Developing assertiveness involves expressing your thoughts and needs confidently while respecting others. This can be particularly challenging in environments where women's voices are marginalized, but as a leader, you need to remove all emotion from the discussion, so you can be objective and collaborative. Start by practicing clear and direct communication. Use "I" statements to express your feelings and needs without sounding accusatory. For instance, say, "I feel overlooked when my ideas are dismissed. I would appreciate more consideration of my input." Additionally, learn to set boundaries and say no when necessary. Assertiveness doesn't mean being aggressive; it means standing up for yourself in a respectful manner. Over time, this approach can help dismantle stereotypes and promote a more equitable environment.

Let's illustrate these techniques with examples. Consider Maria, a mid-level manager in a tech company. She realized her achievements were often overshadowed by her male colleagues'. Maria began documenting her successes and regularly updated her supervisor during one-on-one meetings. She also broadened her network by collaborating with colleagues from different departments. These efforts led to her being considered for a leadership development program. In a separate instance, when negotiating her salary, Maria presented detailed market research and highlighted her contributions to the company's profitability. Her well-prepared case earned her a substantial raise. Lastly, Maria practiced assertiveness by addressing instances where she felt her ideas were dismissed in meetings. She approached her manager and expressed her concerns directly, which resulted in more inclusive discussions moving forward.

Similarly, let's look at Emily, a young entrepreneur. Emily faced numerous biases while pitching her startup. She formed alliances with other female founders and industry veterans who supported each other's ventures. This network provided valuable feedback and opened doors to potential investors. When negotiating terms with an investor, Emily confidently presented her business plan and demonstrated its potential growth, securing favorable terms. Furthermore, Emily took assertiveness training to improve her communication skills. She learned to articulate her vision and needs effectively, helping her gain respect and consideration from stakeholders. Think about women you admire in business. What behaviors and skills are they displaying that you would like to adopt? How can you develop those skills? Have you thought about networking with these women?

Handling Difficult Situations

Navigating gender bias and stereotypes in the workplace often presents significant challenges, especially for women aiming to ascend to leadership roles or manage their businesses effectively. This section provides practical techniques to empower readers to handle these difficult situations pragmatically and confidently.

Conflict Resolution Strategies

Conflicts related to gender biases can arise in many ways, from exclusionary practices to overt discrimination. Addressing these conflicts requires a multifaceted approach tailored to specific scenarios. One effective strategy is to adopt a collaborative conflict resolution style, which involves working together to find mutually beneficial solutions. This approach fosters an environment of inclusivity and respect by ensuring all parties feel heard and valued. Additionally, formal training in mediation can be invaluable. Mediation skills help individuals facilitate discussions between conflicting parties objectively.

For instance, understanding how to de-escalate emotionally charged situations through calm and measured responses can prevent minor issues from becoming significant conflicts. Utilizing role-playing exercises in training settings can prepare individuals to navigate real-life scenarios more effectively.

> **Success Strategy**: Engage proactively in conflict resolution by identifying potential sources of bias-related tension early. Recognize signs such as exclusion from important meetings or unequal distribution of tasks and address them promptly through structured conversations focused on collaborative problem-solving.

Emotional Regulation Techniques

The ability to regulate one's emotions is crucial when facing gender bias in business and in life, which can trigger frustration, anger, or discouragement. Emotional regulation techniques enable individuals to maintain their composure and respond thoughtfully rather than react impulsively.

Mindfulness practices, such as deep breathing and meditation, can help reduce stress and improve emotional control. For example, taking a few minutes to practice deep breathing before a challenging conversation can help center your thoughts and provide clarity. Additionally, regular mindfulness meditation can build long-term resilience against stressors associated with gender bias.

Cognitive reappraisal, a technique where you change your thought patterns about a situation, can also be effective. Instead of viewing a biased comment as a personal attack, reframe it as an opportunity to educate and promote awareness. This shift in perspective reduces negative emotional impact and allows for more constructive engagement.

> **Success Strategy**: Incorporate daily mindfulness practices and cognitive reappraisal techniques into your routine to enhance your ability to manage emotions under pressure. Regularly reflect on challenging interactions to identify emotional triggers and develop healthier responses.

Cultural Intelligence

Developing cultural intelligence (CQ) is essential for understanding and navigating diverse perspectives and biases in the workplace. CQ encompasses the ability to recognize and understand different cultural norms and values and adjust one's behavior accordingly.

To build CQ, immerse yourself in diverse environments and seek interactions with colleagues from various cultural backgrounds. Attend workshops on cultural competence and participate in activities that promote cross-cultural understanding. For example, joining employee resource groups or diversity councils can provide insights into different cultural experiences and challenges within the organization.

Moreover, learning about the cultural dimensions that influence workplace behaviors, such as individualism versus collectivism or high-context versus low-context communication styles, can help anticipate and mitigate potential biases. Understanding these dimensions enables more effective collaboration and conflict resolution in multicultural settings.

> **Success Strategy**: Actively pursue opportunities to enhance your cultural intelligence by engaging with diverse groups, attending relevant training sessions, and educating yourself about cultural dimensions that impact workplace dynamics.

Communication Skills

Effective communication is key to addressing and mitigating bias-related conflicts constructively. Developing strong communication skills can help articulate concerns clearly and assertively while fostering an open dialogue. Active listening is a fundamental aspect of effective communication. As you read earlier, it involves fully concentrating, understanding, responding, and remembering what is being said. By practicing active listening, you demonstrate respect and empathy, making it easier to address biases without escalating tensions. Techniques like paraphrasing the speaker's message and asking clarifying questions can show you value their perspective.

Another critical skill is assertive communication, which strikes a balance between passivity and aggression. Assertiveness involves expressing your needs and opinions confidently and respectfully. For instance, using "I" statements can help convey your feelings without sounding accusatory. Instead of saying, "You are always excluding me from meetings," try, "I feel overlooked when I'm not included in meetings." Collaborative communication strategies, such as joint problem-solving, encourage a team-oriented approach to resolving biases. These strategies involve discussing issues openly and working together to create inclusive solutions. Establishing clear, inclusive guidelines for team interactions can further support this collaborative environment.

> **Success Strategy**: Enhance your communication skills through active listening, assertive expression, and collaborative problem-solving. Participate in communication workshops and practice these techniques in everyday interactions to build confidence and effectiveness.

Closing Remarks

This chapter has delved into the various tactics women can use to overcome gender bias and stereotypes in the workplace. By understanding and recognizing implicit biases, women can begin to challenge these subconscious prejudices head-on. Self-promotion skills, building allies, and developing assertiveness are critical techniques for navigating biased environments. Combining these strategies with effective negotiation skills ensures that women can advocate for themselves confidently and constructively.

These methods help create a more inclusive workplace where women can thrive and advance. In Chapter 6, we'll be exploring how you can develop resilience to adapt to the various challenges you'll face as you climb the career ladder. Your mindset can make or break you, so it is vital that you look at the obstacles in your way as opportunities to grow. When you can view setbacks as learning experiences, you'll be able to navigate adversity with optimism and strength.

Chapter 6:
Developing Resilience and Adaptability

My best successes came on the heels of failures. –Barbara Corcoran

For women aspiring to leadership positions or venturing into entrepreneurship, developing resilience and adaptability can transform obstacles into opportunities for growth. This chapter delves into practical strategies that empower women to foster resilience and adaptability in their personal and professional lives.

As you read further, you will explore how cultivating a growth mindset allows one to turn setbacks into valuable lessons. The importance of seeking feedback and continuously improving oneself will be highlighted, showing how external perspectives can illuminate paths for enhancement. You'll learn ways to interpret obstacles into stepping stones, adopting creative problem-solving techniques to keep moving forward. By maintaining an optimistic outlook and practicing gratitude, the chapter demonstrates how to stay motivated and focused despite challenges. This journey toward resilience and adaptability promises to offer empowering insights that can lead to thriving in dynamic and ever-changing environments.

Cultivating a Growth Mindset

Embracing challenges as learning opportunities is a fundamental shift in mindset that empowers you to see setbacks not as failures, but as valuable experiences that foster growth and improvement. This perspective allows you to navigate adversities with optimism and resilience. For aspiring women leaders and female entrepreneurs, understanding that challenges are inherent to growth can be transformative. Instead of avoiding difficult situations or viewing them as insurmountable obstacles, seeing them as essential components of their journey can foster a healthier, more constructive approach to personal and professional development. One practical way to implement this mindset is by reflecting on past experiences where overcoming difficulties led to significant learning moments. Using the Discovery Journal or any journal to document these instances will serve as a powerful reminder of the positive outcomes that can arise from challenging circumstances.

Seeking feedback and continuous improvement is another critical strategy for developing resilience and adaptability. Engaging actively with feedback, whether from colleagues, mentors, or clients, provides invaluable insights into areas needing enhancement. This proactive approach to self-improvement aligns with the principle that growth is an ongoing process, requiring dedication and openness to learn from others.

Incorporating feedback into daily practice means creating an environment where constructive criticism is welcomed and valued. For instance, setting up regular check-ins with team members or peers to solicit their perspectives can lead to a culture of mutual growth and support. Additionally, seeking mentorship from experienced professionals can provide guidance and insights that are instrumental in navigating complex challenges.

By reinterpreting setbacks as opportunities to refine strategies and improve skills, you can approach problems with a problem-solving mindset rather than a defeatist attitude. This approach encourages perseverance and innovation, key qualities in both leadership and entrepreneurship. We will take a deeper look at the hidden opportunities found in failure a little later in this chapter.

Ultimately, adopting a positive outlook in the face of adversity is vital for maintaining resilience during tough times. An optimistic perspective helps you stay focused on potential solutions rather than getting overwhelmed by the severity of the problem. Optimism also fuels motivation, encouraging you to keep pushing forward despite setbacks.

A practical approach to fostering optimism includes practicing gratitude by regularly acknowledging and appreciating the positive aspects of one's life and work. This practice can shift focus away from negativity and toward a more balanced view of circumstances, reinforcing the belief that challenges are temporary and surmountable.

Furthermore, surrounding oneself with like-minded individuals who share a positive outlook can create a supportive community that bolsters collective resilience.

I have a gratitude journal that I carry with me. It is something I can read through when I find myself in a negative headspace. I highly recommend you start your own gratitude journal to give you perspective during the more challenging times in your career. Scarlett Lea has some fantastic gratitude journals you may want to look into.

Here are the steps to get you started:

1. Get a notebook or journal specifically for your gratitude entries. Having a dedicated space to write down what you're grateful for makes it feel more intentional. Set aside a time each time to write in your journal. Some people prefer doing it first thing in the morning, so they start their day off on a positive note, while others like to write in their journal right before bed to calm any negative thoughts and promote a peaceful night's sleep.

2. Start each entry with the date. This is important since you can then track your progress. You'll be surprised how much easier gratitude becomes as time goes along. Over time, you may notice patterns in what you're grateful for and how your perspective changed over time.

3. Write down your statements in a positive and declarative way. For example, I *have a wonderful husband because he always supports me,*

or *I'm grateful that I have a fridge full of food I can use to cook a delicious meal for my family*.

4. Be as specific as possible when you write in your journal. The more detail, the more impactful this practice is.

5. On the days that you find it extremely hard to think about something you're grateful for, keep it simple. *I'm grateful for the ability to breath in fresh air*, or *I'm grateful for waking up this morning*, will do!

We truly have a lot to be thankful for and appreciating even the small things can have a massive impact on your mindset. The journey of cultivating resilience and adaptability is deeply intertwined with the mindset shift toward embracing challenges, seeking feedback, turning obstacles into stepping stones, and maintaining a positive outlook. Each of these elements plays a crucial role in empowering women leaders and entrepreneurs to thrive in dynamic environments and rise above the hurdles they encounter.

Stress Management Techniques

Practicing Mindfulness and Meditation

Mindfulness and meditation are powerful tools to combat stress and improve mental well-being. These practices help you become more aware of your thoughts and feelings, allowing you to manage them effectively. Mindfulness involves staying present in the moment rather than worrying about the past or future. It can be as simple as taking a few deep breaths and focusing on the sensation of the air entering and leaving your lungs. Regular meditation sessions can create a sense of inner calm, making you more resilient to stress.

One practical way to incorporate mindfulness into your daily routine is by setting aside a few minutes each day for meditation. You can start with just five minutes and gradually increase the duration as you become more comfortable. Find a quiet space where you won't be disturbed, sit comfortably, close your eyes, and focus on your breath. Whenever your mind starts to wander, gently bring your attention back to your breathing. Over time, this practice can enhance your ability to stay focused and centered, even in stressful situations. In addition to daily meditation, integrating mindfulness into everyday activities can also be beneficial. For example, try paying full attention to what you're doing when eating or even washing dishes. By fully engaging in these tasks, you can break free from the cycle of stress and anxiety that often accompanies multitasking and scattered attention.

> **Success Strategy**: Mindful walking is a great way to get outdoors and get some Vitamin D. When you're cooped up in your office the whole day, getting out in nature is a wonderful way to press pause and get perspective.

Engaging in Regular Physical Exercise

Physical exercise is another effective strategy for reducing stress and improving mental health. When you engage in regular physical activity, your body releases endorphins, natural mood lifters that can help you feel more relaxed and positive. Exercise can also improve sleep quality, boost self-confidence, and make you less prone to anxiety and depression.

Different types of exercise can suit various preferences and lifestyles, so it's essential to find an activity you enjoy. This could include joining a gym, participating in group fitness classes, or simply incorporating more movement into your daily routine. Walking, jogging, yoga, and strength training are excellent options.

Even small changes, like taking the stairs instead of the elevator or going for a short walk during breaks, can make a significant difference.

> **Success Strategy**: Taking the stairs instead of the elevator is a minor change you can make to add more physical exercise to your day. Let's face it, not everyone has time to go to the gym; life can be very busy. So, find ways to be more active in your day-to-day dealings. Standing instead of sitting at a desk has also grown in popularity; there are even people who work while walking on the treadmill. How far you take your fitness is up to you but a few hours in the day shouldn't hold you back.

Establishing Boundaries for Work-Life Harmony

Balancing work and personal life is crucial for maintaining mental well-being. Establishing clear boundaries helps prevent burnout and ensures you allocate time for relaxation and self-care. In today's hyper-connected world, it's easy to blur the lines between work and personal life, leading to excessive stress and reduced productivity.

One effective way to establish boundaries is by creating a dedicated workspace if you're working from home. Designating a specific area for work can help you mentally separate professional responsibilities from personal time. Additionally, set specific work hours and stick to them. This means logging off from work emails and communications after a certain time each day, allowing yourself to unwind and recharge.

Another important aspect of maintaining work-life harmony is learning to say no. It's easy to overcommit, especially when striving for success. However, taking on too many responsibilities can lead to exhaustion and decreased performance. Prioritize your tasks and focus on what's most important, delegating or declining additional work when necessary.

Remember that taking care of yourself is vital for long-term success and well-being.

Lisa's Story

It was 2.30 am and I was hunched over my laptop at home. My eyes were tired, my head ached, and my hands were exhausted. This was my life, night after night.

My boss was a tyrant in a tailored suit. He had an insatiable hunger for success and expected his employees to deliver it to him on a silver platter no matter what the cost. I always felt like I was walking on eggshells around him. Not to mention I was an easy target. Not only was I a woman in a male-dominated industry, but I was fresh out of college. I was eager to please and didn't have the ability to say no. My boss exploited that. He piled on the work, the deadlines, and his impossible expectations, and I accepted it. My life was consumed by the demands of my job. Not only did my relationships suffer, but my health was slowly deteriorating.

One day, I stared into a mirror and a pale, haggard woman who looked beyond defeated looked back at me. It was then that I realized this wasn't the life that I wanted. So, I decided to fight back. I learned to say no and set clear boundaries. I put my foot down and refused to let work bleed into every aspect of my phone. Work hours were exactly that, and that's where it stayed. My boss wasn't pleased but I held my ground. Slowly, things began to change at the office. It's as if my boss respected me more. Of course, that wasn't the best of it; I rediscovered myself again. I started sleeping again, eating healthy meals, and reconnecting with my friends and family.

It wasn't an overnight transformation. There were setbacks, moments of doubt, and times when I wanted to give up. But I persevered, and with each passing day, I felt stronger, more confident, and more in control. Today, I am a different person. I am still ambitious, driven, and dedicated to my work. But I am also aware of my worth, my boundaries, and the importance of balance. I am no longer anybody's puppet.

I learned the hard way that saying no is not a sign of weakness, but a sign of strength. It's about respecting yourself, your time, and your well-being. It's about taking control of your life and refusing to be defined by the expectations of others.

> So, if you find yourself in a similar situation, remember, you are not alone. You have the power to break free. Set your boundaries, prioritize your well-being, and never let anyone, not even your boss, dim your light. Your life is precious, and it's time you started living it on your own terms.

Seeking Support Networks and Resources

By now, you know that developing a support network is essential for your success as a leader. Surrounding yourself with supportive individuals can provide a sense of belonging and reduce feelings of isolation. Whether it's friends, family, colleagues, or support groups, having people you can talk to and rely on can significantly impact your resilience.

Reaching out to others doesn't always come naturally, but it's important to recognize when you need help and to ask for it. This can involve confiding in a trusted friend or family member about what you're going through or seeking professional help from a therapist or counselor. Online forums and support groups can also offer valuable connections and advice from people who understand your experiences.

Overall, combining mindfulness, physical exercise, clear boundaries, and a solid support network can create a robust foundation for coping with stress and maintaining mental well-being. These strategies not only help you navigate current challenges but also build resilience for future ones, empowering you to thrive in both your personal and professional life.

Learning From Failures

Setbacks and failures are often seen as stumbling blocks, yet they hold immense value as learning opportunities. They're opportunities for us to check and adjust. Emphasizing the importance of these experiences can transform our approach to challenges, fostering growth and resilience.

Analyzing mistakes for growth insights is crucial in this transformation. By examining past failures, you can uncover lessons that guide your future endeavors. This process starts with honest reflection. It's about asking critical questions like *What went wrong?* and *What could have been done differently?* Such introspection allows you to identify the root causes of setbacks and understand where improvements can be made. For instance, a business owner who faced a failed product launch might analyze customer feedback to discover market misalignment or marketing strategy flaws. These insights can then inform better decisions and strategies moving forward, turning a past failure into a stepping stone for future success. Another vital aspect is embracing resilience in the face of adversity. Resilience isn't just about bouncing back; it's about developing a mindset that sees setbacks as temporary and surmountable. When faced with adversity, resilient individuals maintain optimism and perseverance.

They view each setback as an opportunity to grow stronger and more capable. Consider a leader whose project has failed due to unforeseen challenges. Instead of being demoralized, they take the experience in stride, adapt their strategies, and emerge more resourceful. Resilience in leadership not only aids personal recovery but also inspires and motivates teams to keep pushing forward despite obstacles.

Seeking feedback and self-improvement is a practical guideline that further supports growth from failures. Feedback provides an external perspective that can highlight blind spots and areas needing improvement that we might miss on our own. Asking for constructive criticism requires humility and openness, but it's invaluable for continuous development. For example, a female entrepreneur might solicit feedback from her mentors after a failed business pitch. This input can reveal specific skills she needs to refine, whether it's her presentation style or her understanding of market dynamics. Utilizing such feedback, she can tailor her efforts to address these gaps, enhancing her overall leadership abilities.

Adopting a growth-oriented perspective is essential in recognizing that failures are integral parts of the journey toward success. This mindset shift involves seeing setbacks not as dead ends but as part of the iterative process of learning and improvement. Each failure becomes a valuable lesson that informs and shapes future actions. For instance, let's say you're a corporate leader aiming to break the glass ceiling.

It's very likely that you'll face numerous setbacks along the way. Instead of viewing these as insurmountable barriers, you must understand that each failure offers insights that bring you closer to your goal. This perspective fosters persistence and encourages experimentation, which are crucial for innovation and long-term success.

The narrative of personal growth through failure is enriched by real-life examples. Successful leaders like Oprah Winfrey and J. K. Rowling faced significant setbacks early in their careers but used those experiences as fuel for their eventual triumphs. Their stories illustrate how resilience, coupled with a growth mindset, transforms failures into milestones on the path to success. This narrative is particularly inspiring for aspiring female leaders, showcasing that persistence and adaptability are key components of leadership.

Maintaining Work-Life Balance

Balancing professional demands with personal well-being is crucial for sustained resilience and adaptability. It ensures that, while striving for career success, one does not compromise on health or happiness.

Setting Priorities and Boundaries

Identifying and prioritizing key tasks allows you to focus on what truly matters, preventing the chaos of trying to tackle everything at once. An effective way to prioritize is by using the Eisenhower Matrix which helps classify tasks based on urgency and importance. For instance, addressing a looming project deadline is both urgent and important, whereas regular team meetings may be important but not necessarily urgent. Setting clear boundaries between work and personal life is equally essential. This can mean designating specific hours for work and non-work activities or physically separating workspace from relaxation areas. In collaboration with Scarlett Lea, I have created a Priority Journal called *Decisive Leadership* to support your journey using the Eisenhower Matrix.

Let's have a closer look at the Eisenhower Matrix.

Also known as the Urgent-Important Matrix, this time management and prioritization tool helps individuals and teams organize their tasks and activities based on the principles of importance and urgency.

The Eisenhower Matrix consists of four quadrants:

1. **Urgent and Important (Do)**: Tasks that are both urgent and important, such as pressing deadlines or crises. These tasks require immediate attention and should be completed as soon as possible.

2. **Not Urgent but Important (Schedule)**: Tasks that are important but not urgent, such as long-term projects, personal development, or strategic planning. These tasks should be scheduled and given dedicated time and attention to ensure they are completed.

3. **Urgent but Not Important (Delegate)**: Tasks that are urgent but not particularly important, such as interruptions, phone calls, or unexpected requests. These tasks should be delegated to others or handled in a more efficient manner, such as by setting boundaries or limiting the time spent on them.

4. **Not Urgent and Not Important (Eliminate)**: Tasks that are neither urgent nor important, such as browsing social media, watching TV, or engaging in unproductive activities. These tasks

should be eliminated or minimized to free up time and focus on more productive and meaningful activities.

The Eisenhower Matrix helps to distinguish between what is truly important and what is merely urgent, allowing for better time and resource allocation.

The key benefits of using the Eisenhower Matrix include:

- Increased productivity and efficiency by focusing on high-impact activities. Improved decision-making by distinguishing between important and urgent tasks.

- Better time management by delegating or eliminating low-value activities.

- Reduced stress and burnout by prioritizing long-term goals and personal development.

Scheduling Self-Care Activities

Allocating regular time for self-care and leisure activities is indispensable for your overall health and should be non-negotiable in your schedule. The mantra "You cannot pour from an empty cup" underscores the importance of self-care. Whether it's a daily exercise regimen, weekend hobbies, or simple relaxation practices like reading or meditating, dedicating time for yourself recharges your mental and physical batteries. Once a month, I go to the spa and get a massage; this helps with stress and relaxation. Effective self-care often requires putting it on your calendar just as you would any other important meeting or task. If you use digital calendars, set reminders to take short breaks throughout your day. Short breaks improve focus and prevent the fatigue that long periods of concentrated work can bring. Additionally, engaging in activities that bring joy and relaxation can serve as a buffer against stress.

> **Success Strategy**: Taking a long, hot bath after a busy day at the office is a form of self-care that's often overlooked. Light a candle, put on your favorite music, and soak in the tub to help relax your muscles and mind.

Delegating Responsibilities and Empowering Others

One of the critical aspects of maintaining balance is recognizing that you do not have to do everything yourself. Effective delegation is vital for avoiding overload and encouraging teamwork. Start by identifying tasks that can be handled by others and trust your team to execute them. Delegation not only alleviates your burden but also empowers others to grow and develop new skills.

Empowering your team by delegating responsibilities can foster a collaborative work environment. Trusting others with important tasks can boost their confidence and competence, making them feel valued. It's important to provide clear instructions and necessary resources when delegating. Regular check-ins can ensure that the tasks are progressing as expected without needing to micromanage. Delegating in your personal life shouldn't be forgotten! Hiring a cleaning lady or someone to help in the garden can take a lot of pressure off you.

Moreover, fostering a culture where everyone feels comfortable taking on new challenges can enhance overall team performance. Research has shown that distributing responsibilities effectively not only prevents individual burnout but also promotes a sense of ownership and involvement among team members (Kalev & Dobbin, 2022). We'll take a closer look at the power of delegation in a later chapter.

Establishing Healthy Habits and Routines

Integrating healthy habits and routines into daily life can significantly impact both your physical and mental well-being. Simple habits like maintaining a balanced diet, getting adequate sleep, and practicing regular physical activity can contribute immensely to your energy levels and overall health. It's beneficial to create routines that incorporate these elements seamlessly into your daily life.

For instance, starting your day with a nutritious breakfast, allocating specific times for meals, and ensuring you drink enough water are basic yet impactful habits. Likewise, establishing a consistent sleep schedule can enhance productivity and mood. You may want to look at Scarlett Lea's journal called Mindful Metris: Wellness One Day At a Time where you'll be able to track healthy habits like sleep, water intake, diet/weight, energy, and exercise. Physical exercises such as yoga, walking, or any preferred workout should be scheduled regularly. These habits are not time-consuming but profoundly affect how you feel and perform in both professional and personal spheres.

Summary and Reflections

Building resilience means seeing challenges as opportunities to learn and grow. It's about changing how you think about setbacks, viewing them as steps that help you improve rather than as failures. By reflecting on past experiences where you've overcome difficulties, you can appreciate the value of these moments in shaping your journey. Seeking feedback and continuously working on self-improvement are key strategies. Engaging with others' perspectives provides insights into areas you might overlook, helping you become more adaptable and resilient over time. Turning obstacles into stepping stones is essential for growth. Reinterpreting setbacks as chances to refine our strategies fosters a problem-solving mindset. Celebrating small victories reinforces the belief that each challenge contributes to progress. Adopting a positive outlook helps you stay focused on finding solutions, fueling your motivation even when times are tough. Surrounding yourself with supportive individuals who share this mindset can create a strong community that encourages mutual growth. Through perseverance and optimism, women leaders and entrepreneurs can thrive, turning every obstacle into an opportunity for success. If you're in the mood for some extra reading, I highly recommend the *Happy Habits* series by Elizabeth

Bright. *Happy Habits*, *12 Months of Happy Habits*, as well as *Work Life Balance* are books that taught me how to juggle my personal and professional life successfully.

In the next chapter, we're going to look into verbal and non-verbal communication. The ability to communicate effectively is a great way to enhance your leadership capabilities. Let's look at everything from active listening to understanding body language can improve your communication skills.

Chapter 7:
Mastering Communication Skills

Ninety percent of leadership is the ability to communicate something people want. –
Dianne Feinstein

This chapter delves into both verbal and non-verbal aspects of communication—skills that are essential for anyone aspiring to lead, influence, and inspire. From understanding the nuances of body language to developing active listening practices, this chapter offers a comprehensive guide to improving communication.

Throughout this chapter, you will explore various techniques and strategies to refine your communication style. You'll learn about the significance of body language in projecting confidence and authority, as well as how different cultures interpret non-verbal cues.

The chapter also discusses the importance of tailoring your communication style to resonate with diverse audiences. Additionally, it emphasizes the role of active listening in fostering collaboration and trust within teams.

By integrating these skills, leaders can create an environment of mutual respect and cooperation, ultimately guiding their teams toward shared success.

Verbal and Non-Verbal Communication

Effective leadership hinges on the dual pillars of verbal and non-verbal communication. These facets of communication, when mastered, significantly enhance your ability to inspire, influence, and guide your team toward achieving common goals.

Understanding Body Language

Communication is much more than just words spoken or written; it's also deeply embedded in non-verbal cues. Research by UCLA professor Albert Mehrabian suggests that a substantial portion of communication, as much as 55%, is conveyed through body language (Camarote, 2023). This underscores the importance for leaders to be adept at interpreting and using these cues effectively.

Non-verbal communication includes facial expressions, gestures, posture, eye contact, and even subtle movements, all of which convey messages about confidence, emotions, and intentions. For instance, nodding can indicate agreement and attentiveness, while crossed arms may signal defensiveness or disinterest. Since your face reflects your emotions, it is important to train yourself to keep it neutral and relaxed, even under pressure. You should also be mindful that pointing is a big no-no in Western culture, so always use broad hand gestures. By learning to read and understand these cues, leaders can better gauge the sentiments and reactions of their team members, leading to more effective interactions.

Utilizing Body Language to Convey Confidence and Authority

A key aspect of successful leadership is projecting confidence and authority. Non-verbal cues play an essential role in this projection. Simple adjustments, like standing tall with shoulders back, maintaining steady eye contact, and using open gestures, can make a significant difference in how a leader is perceived. When you exhibit confident body language, it not only enhances your own presence but also instills confidence in your team.

For example, consider a leader giving a presentation. Standing upright, making purposeful hand gestures, and maintaining consistent eye contact can capture and retain the audience's attention far more effectively than slouching, fidgeting, or avoiding eye contact. These non-verbal signals communicate that you're both knowledgeable and capable, encouraging others to trust and follow your lead.

> **Success Strategy**: Always keep your body open to make your audience feel at ease. This means not crossing your arms or legs. Your body should also be positioned toward the person you're talking to. This openness makes you come across as more trustworthy.

Tailoring Communication Style to Resonate With Diverse Audiences

Effective communication in leadership isn't one-size-fits-all. You must be adept at tailoring your communication styles to connect with a diverse range of individuals. This involves understanding cultural nuances and different personality types to ensure messages are received and interpreted as intended. Different cultures have various interpretations of non-verbal behaviors. For instance, in some cultures, direct eye contact signifies confidence and honesty, while in others, it might be seen as disrespectful or confrontational. Recognizing these differences allows leaders to adapt their approach to avoid miscommunication and foster better relationships.

Additionally, communication styles must also align with individual preferences and roles within a team. Some team members may respond better to detailed, data-driven discussions, while others might prefer high-level overviews with visual aids. Tailoring communication to suit these preferences ensures that everyone remains engaged and informed, ultimately enhancing team cohesion and productivity.

Utilizing Active Listening to Foster Understanding and Collaboration

As you've read throughout this book, active listening is foundational in effective communication and crucial for building trust and fostering collaboration within teams. It's not merely about hearing words but fully comprehending the underlying messages and emotions being conveyed. This skill involves techniques such as providing undivided attention, reflecting on what's been said, and responding thoughtfully. A favorite quote of mine is by South African advocate, Thuli Madonsela: "I need to listen well so that I hear what is not said." Active listening demonstrates a leader's genuine interest in their team members' perspectives, concerns, and ideas. It involves validating their contributions and addressing any issues raised promptly and empathetically. Leaders who practice active listening create an environment where team members feel valued and understood, which is essential for fostering a collaborative culture.

Practical Guidelines for Enhancing Non-Verbal Communication

- **Mirror Practice**: Spend a few minutes each day practicing different facial expressions and postures in front of a mirror. This helps in becoming more aware of the non-verbal messages you send.

- **Film Yourself**: Record yourself during mock meetings or presentations to gain insights into your body language habits. This can reveal areas for improvement in your non-verbal communication.

- **Maintain Eye Contact**: Consistent and comfortable eye contact shows attentiveness and interest. It's a simple yet powerful way to engage with your audience.

- **Avoid Distractions**: Put away distractions like phones during conversations to give your full attention to the speaker, demonstrating respect and genuine interest.

By integrating these practices, you can refine your non-verbal communication skills, thus enhancing your overall executive presence. Effective verbal and non-verbal communication is integral to successful leadership. Leaders who can convey their vision clearly, project confidence through their body language, tailor their communication to their audience, and actively listen to their team create an environment of mutual respect and collaboration. As they master these skills, they become more inspiring and influential, guiding their teams toward shared success.

Negotiation Skills

Preparation for Negotiations

Effective preparation is a cornerstone of successful negotiation. If you're aiming for a leadership position or plan on running your own business, mastering the art of negotiation begins long before entering the meeting room. Preparation involves thorough research about the subject matter, understanding the needs and interests of the other party, and setting clear, achievable objectives.

Research is critical in negotiations as it arms you with essential information that can enhance your bargaining power. For example, if you're negotiating a salary increase, research industry salary standards, your company's financial health, and your achievements that justify the raise.

Utilize resources such as industry reports, company financial statements, and professional networks to gather relevant data. This diligent preparation ensures that you are well-informed and confident when presenting your case, making it difficult for the other party to refute your arguments. Setting clear objectives is equally important.

Define what you aim to achieve from the negotiation. These goals must be specific, measurable, attainable, relevant, and time-bound (SMART). For instance, instead of vague objectives like "get a higher salary," specify the exact amount or percentage increase you desire.

Additionally, consider the best and worst outcomes you can accept. Such clarity helps in maintaining focus during the discussions, preventing deviations from your primary goals. Scarlett Lea has weekly/monthly/quarterly journals to support setting clear objectives using SMART goals.

I suggest you look into these journals as they allow space for key actions and notes, which is very helpful.

Managing Conflict and Reaching Mutually Beneficial Agreements

Negotiation often entails managing conflict and seeking resolutions that benefit all parties involved. As a woman, you're uniquely positioned to excel in this arena due to your natural aptitude for fostering collaboration and communication. Instead of viewing conflicts as negative obstacles, it's vital to see them as opportunities for creative problem-solving. A key strategy in managing conflict is active listening. Paying close attention to the concerns and interests of the other party allows for a deeper understanding, which can pave the way for finding common ground.

One practical approach is to frame the negotiation as a partnership rather than a confrontation. Emphasize shared goals and how achieving these objectives can be mutually beneficial. For example, if negotiating a business partnership, highlight how collaboration can lead to greater market reach and increased profits for both parties. Approach each discussion with the intent of finding win-win solutions, where both sides feel they have gained something valuable.

> **Success Strategy**: Conflict isn't always a bad thing. It can teach you a lot about the other person and may improve your relationship. How? Conflict highlights areas that need to be worked on, which can spark collaboration. Don't shy away from conflict. Stand your ground but always be fair.

Overcoming Gender Biases in Negotiation Settings

Despite progress toward gender equality, women can still face biases and stereotypes that affect their negotiation experiences. Myths such as women being less effective negotiators persist, creating undue pressure and sometimes leading to self-doubt. Overcoming these biases requires a multi-faceted approach. First, confidence is essential. Believe in your worth and capabilities, and do not hesitate to assert yourself firmly but politely. Occupying physical space confidently can also help establish a position of power. Arriving early to meetings, taking a seat at the table, and maintaining good posture can project authority and boost self-assurance. Also, be sure to greet people as they arrive—own the room! Power poses can significantly bolster your confidence during negotiations. I also want you to be okay with pauses or silence. There's no need for you to fill the silence during negotiations; instead, be comfortable in these quiet moments as it shows you're confident in what you're asking for.

Second, be aware of and address any unconscious biases that may arise. Prepare to counteract stereotypes by providing evidence of your expertise and past successes. Demonstrating your value through concrete examples can dispel doubts and build credibility. Lastly, foster alliances and seek mentorship from other women who have successfully navigated similar challenges. Sharing experiences and strategies can empower women and provide practical insights into overcoming gender biases. Engaging in women's leadership programs can also enhance negotiation skills and offer a supportive community. You should also look into taking a negotiation class.

Leveraging Emotional Intelligence for Successful Negotiation Outcomes

Emotional intelligence (EQ) plays a crucial role in negotiation, influencing how we perceive and manage our emotions and those of others. Women often possess strong EQ, giving them an edge in understanding and navigating the emotional landscape of negotiations.

One aspect of leveraging EQ is balancing assertiveness with empathy. Being assertive is necessary to advocate for one's goals, but coupling it with empathy ensures that assertiveness is perceived positively rather than as bossiness. Empathizing with the other party involves recognizing their feelings, motivations, and constraints. This understanding can help tailor your approach to address their concerns effectively, fostering goodwill and collaboration.

For example, if negotiating a flexible work arrangement, acknowledge the company's operational needs and propose solutions that meet both your personal needs and the organization's requirements. By showing empathy, you demonstrate that you value the other party's perspective, which can lead to more cooperative and productive discussions.

Another aspect of EQ involves managing stress and staying calm under pressure. Negotiations can be emotionally taxing, often involving extended discussions and potential setbacks. Developing techniques to stay composed—such as deep breathing exercises, taking breaks, and focusing on your objectives—can enhance your ability to make rational decisions and maintain a positive demeanor. Of course, you need to be open to a different outcome than what you hoped for. Flexibility and a fallback position are key during negotiations.

Practice, Practice, Practice

Negotiation skills, like any other skill, require practice to master. Regularly engaging in negotiations, whether in professional settings or everyday life, can build confidence and competence. Practice helps overcome fears and discomfort, making negotiation a more natural and less daunting process.

Start small by negotiating in low-stakes scenarios, such as asking for the military, teacher, AAA discount. What can they say? No? My spouse is a veteran and we get discounts all the time by just showing his DD-214 on our phones. As you gain experience, progressively tackle more significant challenges. Additionally, seek feedback from mentors, colleagues, or negotiation workshops to refine your techniques and learn new strategies.

Public Speaking Tips

Cultivating public speaking skills is crucial for aspiring leaders and entrepreneurs to communicate with impact and influence. Whether presenting a business proposal, addressing a team, or networking at a corporate event, mastering the art of public speaking can significantly elevate one's leadership presence and effectiveness. Overcoming stage fright and developing confidence in public speaking are vital skills. Fear of public speaking is common, but it can be managed and reduced through preparation and practice. Acknowledge that nervousness is normal and can even enhance alertness and performance when harnessed correctly (Saint Leo University, 2021). Practice is essential. Rehearse your speech multiple times, ideally in front of a friend or a camera to receive feedback and make necessary adjustments. Visualization techniques can also help; imagine yourself delivering a successful speech, which can build confidence and reduce anxiety. Additionally, focus on deep breathing exercises before stepping on stage to calm your nerves and center yourself.

> **Success Strategy:** Sharing a personal story can be a great icebreaker. It helps the audience relate to you. Of course, read the room; it's best to keep it lighthearted and if possible, humorous.

Employing voice modulation and body language for impactful presentations adds depth and authenticity to your communication. Your voice is a powerful tool that can convey enthusiasm, urgency, and sincerity. Vary your pitch, tone, and pace to emphasize important points and keep your audience engaged. Avoid a monotonous delivery, as it can quickly lose audience interest.

Similarly, body language plays a critical role in reinforcing your message. Maintain eye contact to create a connection with your audience, use hand gestures to illustrate points, and ensure your posture exudes confidence.

Nervous habits such as fidgeting or avoiding eye contact can detract from your credibility and distract your audience (North, 2020). Personally, I find that using jokes is an effective way to become more comfortable and engage the audience. Give it a try, maybe you'll be surprised how laughter can loosen up a room.

Handling Q&A sessions with poise and clarity is an opportunity to further demonstrate your expertise and engage with your audience. Approach questions with a positive mindset and view them as a chance to deepen the discussion. Listen attentively to each question, ensuring you understand it fully before responding. If needed, repeat or rephrase the question to clarify it for everyone present. Keep your answers concise and to the point, providing relevant information without going off on tangents. Lastly, remember that although you probably know more than anyone else in the room, if you don't know the answer, tell them you'll get back to them on it. It's not a big deal.

Concluding Thoughts

Mastering the art of effective communication is essential for women in leadership and entrepreneurial roles. This chapter has highlighted the significance of both verbal and non-verbal communication. By understanding and utilizing body language, leaders can project confidence and connect more deeply with their audiences. Tailoring communication styles to resonate with diverse individuals ensures that messages are received as intended, enhancing team cohesion and productivity. Active listening plays a pivotal role in building trust and collaboration, enabling leaders to foster an environment where everyone feels heard and valued.

Incorporating these practices into daily interactions can transform the way you inspire and influence your teams. Confidently expressing your ideas through purposeful body language, embracing cultural nuances, and actively listening to others' perspectives create a foundation for strong, effective leadership. As you continue to navigate leadership challenges, these communication skills will be invaluable in forging meaningful connections, resolving conflicts, and driving collective success. By refining your communication abilities, you can empower your teams and achieve shared goals with greater ease and effectiveness.

In Chapter 8, we're going to look at turning you into a visionary leader. We'll explore what exactly visionary leadership entails and the qualities you need to possess to turn this dream into a reality. By the end of the chapter, you'll have a clear vision of what steps you need to take to become a brilliant leader who can take your team to new heights.

Chapter 8:

Visionary Leadership

Leadership is a series of behaviors rather than a role for heroes. –Margaret Wheatley

Visionary leadership is about casting a compelling and motivating picture of the future that aligns with an organization's core values and mission. It's more than just planning; it's the art of connecting deeply with people and drawing them into a shared journey toward a better tomorrow. Visionary leaders illuminate the path ahead, inspiring their teams to reach beyond the immediate challenges and embrace the possibilities that lie ahead. This chapter explores the intricate dynamics of visionary leadership, providing insights into the qualities and actions necessary for transforming visions into reality.

In this chapter, you will delve into the essential components of visionary leadership, starting with how to craft a vision that resonates universally across all levels of an organization. You will learn about setting clear and actionable objectives that keep everyone aligned and motivated toward common goals. Additionally, the chapter discusses the importance of effective communication in ensuring that the vision is understood and embraced by all stakeholders. By incorporating feedback and fostering inclusivity during the vision creation process, visionary leaders can build a robust and adaptable framework. Through practical examples and strategies, this chapter will equip you with the tools needed to inspire and engage your team, driving collective success.

Crafting a Compelling Vision

Creating a clear and inspiring vision for an organization is paramount to successful leadership, but many leaders fail at this. A visionary leader articulates a direction that not only aligns with the organization's mission and values but also resonates deeply with everyone involved. This involves outlining future goals, setting motivating objectives, effectively communicating the vision, and engaging various stakeholders to create a shared framework. Ultimately, leaders at every level should set a clear and inspiring vision. When articulating a vision, it's essential to depict a compelling future. The vision should paint a vivid picture of what the future looks like for the organization. Furthermore, the vision should be clear, aligned with your mission, and aspirational in nature. Similarly, the vision needs to be closely tied to the organization's core values and purpose. A vision misaligned with foundational principles can easily lose credibility and fail to inspire commitment.

Setting clear objectives is crucial. Objectives break down the broader vision into manageable parts that guide daily activities and long-term strategies. These objectives need to be SMART, as we discussed in the previous chapter. By doing so, you provide a clear roadmap for employees, helping them understand their roles in achieving the larger vision. SMART objectives act as milestones that keep the team motivated and focused on the goal. They ensure that each member knows exactly what is expected and can track their progress over time.

Furthermore, engaging employees, customers, and partners in the vision creation process enhances its authenticity and acceptance. When stakeholders feel a part of the vision, they are more likely to internalize it and work toward it passionately. This engagement can happen through brainstorming sessions, surveys, or collaborative workshops. Incorporating diverse perspectives ensures that the vision is well-rounded and robust, reflecting the collective aspirations of the organization.

> **Success Strategy**: To get everyone engaged in creating a vision, have them write a 15-word vision for the organization or group. Next, review all the sentences and circle the words that are used the most. Then craft a new sentence (vision) using these words.

Inclusivity in crafting the vision allows for innovative ideas and diverse viewpoints to emerge, making the vision more comprehensive and resilient. Engaging various stakeholders helps in identifying potential challenges and opportunities that might not be visible from a single vantage point. This holistic approach to visioning not only makes the vision stronger but also more adaptable to changes in the external environment. The essence of visionary leadership lies in the ability to connect the dots between present capabilities and future aspirations. This connection requires a clear articulation of the vision, specific objectives to guide actions, effective communication to foster understanding and support, and inclusive engagement to build a shared and authentic vision. When successfully implemented, this approach not only propels the organization forward but also creates a cohesive and motivated workforce dedicated to achieving common goals.

Strategic Planning

Strategic planning can empower you to accelerate in your career as it provides a structured approach to reaching your vision. By setting clear, measurable goals and identifying the skills needed to achieve them, you can create actionable steps that guide your progress. Strategic planning provides a structured pathway to achieve long-term goals while maintaining alignment with immediate objectives.

One of the foundational tools in strategic planning is the SWOT analysis, which stands for Strengths, Weaknesses, Opportunities, and Threats. This tool helps leaders gain a comprehensive understanding of both internal capabilities and external possibilities. By listing strengths and weaknesses, organizations can capitalize on what they do well and address areas needing improvement. For example, a company might identify its strength in innovative product design but recognize a weakness in its marketing strategy. Simultaneously, exploring opportunities and threats helps anticipate market trends and potential obstacles, ensuring a proactive approach to decision-making. Conducting a SWOT analysis offers a clear framework for strategic planning by situating the organization within its broader context. Performing this exercise on teams, organizations, or even projects will set you apart as a leader. Identifying key initiatives and action plans to bridge the gap between the current state and desired outcomes is another vital component of strategic planning. For example, a tech startup aiming to become a market leader in cybersecurity might identify key initiatives such as expanding its product offering, investing in research and development, and forging strategic partnerships with industry leaders. Each initiative should have a detailed action plan outlining the necessary steps, responsible parties, timelines, and required resources. Action plans serve as roadmaps, guiding the organization's day-to-day activities toward achieving its strategic objectives.

Resource allocation and risk management are paramount in executing strategies effectively. In any organization, resources—whether financial, human, or technological—are limited. Strategic planning ensures these resources are allocated where they can make the most significant impact. For instance, an organization might decide to invest more heavily in digital transformation efforts if that's identified as a key driver of future growth. Managing risks involves anticipating potential obstacles and developing contingency plans.

Creating agile frameworks is essential for maintaining flexibility and allowing for course corrections based on feedback and changing circumstances. In today's fast-paced business environment, the ability to pivot quickly can be a competitive advantage. Agile frameworks, common in software development but applicable across industries, emphasize iterative progress and continuous improvement. For instance, a marketing team using an agile framework might launch a series of small, test campaigns, gathering data and refining their strategies in real-time based on performance metrics. This iterative approach allows organizations to remain responsive and adaptive, continuously aligning their efforts with evolving goals and market conditions.

Encouraging out-of-the-box thinking is another crucial element that supports innovation and growth within the strategic planning process. Leaders should foster an environment where creative ideas are welcomed and explored. This can be facilitated through brainstorming sessions, cross-departmental collaborations, and dedicated innovation labs. For example, Google's famous "20% time" policy encouraged employees to spend 20% of their work time on projects outside their usual responsibilities, leading to the creation of successful products like Gmail and Google Maps. Supporting unconventional thinking helps organizations discover new opportunities and stay ahead of the competition. Fostering an environment that embraces change and continuous improvement further enhances the effectiveness of strategic planning. Change is inevitable, and the ability to adapt swiftly is vital for sustained success. Organizations should promote a culture where feedback is valued, and improvements are continually sought. This can be achieved through regular training programs, performance reviews, and open communication channels. An example of this is Toyota's Kaizen philosophy, which emphasizes continuous, incremental improvements in every aspect of the company. This mindset of ongoing refinement enables organizations to evolve with the market dynamics and improve operational efficiency over time.

Inspiring and Motivating Teams

In the ever-evolving landscape of corporate leadership, visionary leaders are not only forward-thinkers but also adept at rallying their teams to achieve a shared vision. The essence of visionary leadership lies in the ability to inspire and motivate team members toward collective goals. This subpoint explores practical techniques that aspiring leaders can implement to foster a sense of purpose, recognize contributions, celebrate successes, and nurture an inclusive work environment.

Embracing a Transformational Leadership Style

Transformational leadership is pivotal for inspiring teams. This style emphasizes creating a compelling vision and motivating employees by connecting their sense of self to the larger organizational mission. Transformational leaders are adept at fostering an environment where personal growth and professional development are prioritized. By encouraging team members to take ownership of their roles and responsibilities, leaders can instill a deep sense of purpose within their teams. Each member feels valued and recognized for their unique contributions, leading to heightened engagement and productivity.

To implement this style effectively, it's crucial for you to communicate your vision clearly and consistently. Regularly sharing updates on how individual efforts contribute to overarching goals keeps the vision tangible and attainable.

Providing opportunities for continuous learning and development further solidifies the transformational approach. This could include mentorship programs, skill-building workshops, or even cross-departmental experiences to broaden perspectives and enhance competencies.

> **Success Strategy**: Transformational leadership is built on the acceptance of a common vision. Since there usually are no extrinsic rewards to keep team members motivated, it's possible for them to lose faith in the process along the way. This is why effective communication is key. You should keep your team up to date with what's happening, provide them with constructive feedback, and also take the time to listen to their concerns.

Celebrating Achievements and Milestones

Celebrating milestones is a vital technique for maintaining momentum and boosting team morale. By taking the time to acknowledge both small wins and major accomplishments, leaders reinforce the value of persistence and hard work. Celebrations can range from informal gatherings like team lunches to more elaborate events such as award ceremonies or company-wide announcements.

For instance, celebrating the completion of a significant project with a team outing can provide a much-needed break and strengthen interpersonal bonds. Similarly, recognizing service anniversaries with personalized tokens of appreciation can convey that each individual's long-term commitment is valued.

Creating a timeline of key milestones and planning regular celebrations around these points helps embed a culture of recognition and appreciation, making achievements more meaningful and motivating for the team.

Cultivating a Supportive and Inclusive Work Environment

A supportive and inclusive work environment is foundational for fostering collaboration, creativity, and overall well-being among team members. Inclusivity means ensuring that all voices are heard and respected, regardless of background, gender, or position within the company. Leaders can cultivate such an environment by actively promoting diversity and inclusion initiatives, providing equal opportunities for growth, and addressing any form of bias or discrimination promptly.

Encouraging open communication is another critical aspect of inclusivity. Leaders should create channels where team members feel comfortable sharing their ideas, concerns, and feedback without fear of retribution. Regular one-on-one meetings, anonymous suggestion boxes, and open-door policies can facilitate this. Transparent communication regarding organizational changes and decisions also builds trust and reinforces the feeling of being part of a cohesive team.

Supportiveness extends beyond professional realms. Recognizing the importance of work-life balance and providing resources for mental and physical well-being can significantly impact team morale. Flexible working hours, remote work options, wellness programs, and access to mental health services demonstrate a leader's commitment to the holistic well-being of their team members.

Innovative Thinking

Innovative thinking is fundamental to visionary leadership. An effective leader inspires their team to think creatively and look beyond the usual ways of doing things. Cultivating a culture of creativity and experimentation is the first step in driving innovation and growth within an organization. This involves creating an environment where employees feel safe to express new ideas, no matter how unconventional they may seem.

You should encourage brainstorming sessions and provide the tools and resources necessary for team members to explore their creative potential. For example, tech companies like Google have designated "innovation hours," allowing employees to work on any projects they are passionate about. This initiative has led to the creation of many successful products, including Gmail and Google News. By providing space and time for creativity, leaders can unlock hidden talents within their teams and drive organizational growth.

Risk-taking is another crucial component in fostering innovative thinking. Encouraging employees to take calculated risks can lead to breakthrough innovations, but it's essential to create a culture where failure is seen as a learning opportunity rather than a setback. When team members know that their leaders support them, even if they fail, they are more likely to take the bold steps needed to solve complex problems creatively.

A practical approach to encourage risk-taking is using a cost/benefit analysis to assess the potential outcomes of a risky decision. By weighing the pros and cons, you can make informed decisions and guide your teams toward taking prudent risks. For instance, a startup might decide to invest in cutting-edge technology despite the initial costs, knowing that the long-term benefits could disrupt the market and establish them as industry leaders. Learning from both successes and failures ensures continuous improvement and cultivates an innovative mindset.

> **Success Strategy**: Create an environment where your team members feel safe and they will be more open to taking calculated risks.

Staying abreast of emerging technologies and industry trends is another critical aspect of encouraging innovative thinking. In today's fast-paced world, keeping up with technological advancements and market shifts is essential for remaining competitive. Visionary leaders invest time in researching and understanding new tools and techniques that can improve their business operations. Additionally, you should encourage your team to engage in continuous learning. Creating opportunities for employees to attend workshops, webinars, and training sessions keeps them informed about the latest industry trends and equips them with new skills. For example, a marketing team might benefit from a workshop on the latest digital marketing strategies, allowing them to implement cutting-edge techniques in their campaigns.

Bringing It All Together

In this chapter, we've explored the essence of visionary leadership and how to inspire others to follow. We discussed the importance of crafting a clear vision that aligns with organizational values while also painting an aspirational picture of the future. This chapter made it clear that a compelling vision can drive unity and motivation within an organization. Setting SMART objectives allows for tangible progress, ensuring each team member understands their role in achieving the broader vision. Effective communication and inclusive engagement were emphasized as crucial elements in gaining buy-in from all stakeholders and fostering a shared sense of purpose.

Moreover, engaging various stakeholders in the vision creation process enriches its authenticity and acceptance. We briefly touched on the 15-word vision exercise where all stakeholders get a chance to give their input. By incorporating diverse perspectives, leaders create a vision that is both comprehensive and adaptable to changes in the external environment. Ultimately, visionary leadership connects present capabilities with future aspirations by clearly articulating the vision, setting specific objectives, effectively communicating, and inclusively engaging everyone involved. This cohesive approach not only propels organizations forward but also nurtures a motivated and united workforce dedicated to common goals.

As we move on, it's now time to explore practical strategies for effective delegation. In the next chapter, you'll learn how to analyze tasks to match them with the right team member, how to provide clear instructions, and finally, how to maintain regular check-ins to ensure smooth progress.

Chapter 9:
Delegation and Trust-Building

People become motivated when you guide them to the source of their own power and when you make heroes out of employees who personify what you want to see in the organization. –Anita Roddick

Mastering the art of delegation is a vital skill for any leader, as it not only lightens their workload but also fosters growth and engagement within the team. Effective delegation goes beyond simply distributing tasks; it involves empowering team members by entrusting them with responsibilities that challenge their abilities and build their confidence. When leaders delegate successfully, they create an environment where employees feel valued and motivated to contribute their best efforts, ultimately driving the team's collective success.

In this chapter, we will also examine how building trust within your team through authenticity, transparency, consistency, and accountability can significantly boost morale and productivity. By the end of this chapter, you will have a comprehensive understanding of how to delegate tasks efficiently while cultivating a trusting and cohesive team dynamic.

Importance of Delegation

Effective delegation is a cornerstone of strong leadership, significantly impacting team efficiency and growth. By understanding the importance of delegating tasks, leaders can cultivate an environment where team members feel empowered, skillful, and engaged. One crucial aspect of delegation is its ability to empower team members. When leaders delegate tasks, they not only share responsibilities but also provide team members with opportunities to take ownership and demonstrate their capabilities.

This sense of ownership can be immensely motivating, as employees feel trusted and valued. For example, consider a project manager who assigns a key task to a junior team member. This action signals trust and belief in the employee's ability to manage important aspects of the project. As a result, the employee becomes more invested in the outcome, striving to meet or exceed expectations. Empowerment through delegation fosters a culture of shared responsibility, where each team member understands that their contributions are vital to the team's success. This approach not only enhances individual confidence but also encourages a proactive attitude toward problem-solving and innovation. As team members grow more confident in their abilities, they are likely to take on greater challenges independently, ultimately contributing to the overall efficiency of the team.

Another significant benefit of delegation is improved time management for leaders. By entrusting tasks to capable team members, you can focus on your strategic responsibilities and the broader vision of the organization. This shift allows you to allocate your time more effectively, concentrating on high-level decision-making and long-term planning. For instance, a CEO who delegates routine operational tasks to their team can dedicate more time to developing new business strategies, exploring market opportunities, and strengthening relationships with key stakeholders.

Effective time management through delegation also prevents you from becoming overwhelmed by the minutiae of daily operations. Instead of getting bogged down by routine tasks, you can maintain a clearer perspective on the organization's goals and direction, ensuring that your efforts align with the overall mission. This strategic focus not only leads to better decision-making but also sets a positive example for the team, demonstrating the importance of prioritizing and managing time efficiently.

> **Success Strategy**: For those who struggle to delegate, there's a feeling of "What if?" What if they don't do it correctly or at all? To overcome this, you need to challenge your own assumptions. One way to do this is to start small; assign minor projects to see whether your feelings about delegation are true or only a desire to protect yourself.

Delegation is equally important for skill development within a team. By assigning tasks that challenge employees, leaders create opportunities for growth and learning. These delegated tasks serve as practical training experiences, allowing team members to develop new skills and expand their knowledge. For example, when a senior leader delegates a complex project to a less experienced colleague, the colleague gains hands-on experience in project management, problem-solving, and decision-making.

Effective communication is a critical component of successful delegation. Clear and concise communication ensures that tasks are understood and executed efficiently. You must clearly articulate the desired outcomes, deadlines, and any specific requirements associated with the delegated tasks.

For instance, a marketing director delegating the creation of a campaign plan should provide detailed guidelines on the target audience, key messages, and expected deliverables.

Proper communication also involves setting expectations and providing context for the delegated tasks. When employees understand the significance of their assignments and how they contribute to the larger goals of the organization, they are more likely to approach their work with a sense of purpose and dedication. Additionally, open lines of communication allow team members to seek clarification, ask questions, and receive feedback throughout the process, ensuring that any potential issues are addressed promptly.

Techniques for Effective Delegation

Effective delegation is essential for enhancing team productivity and cohesion. By mastering practical strategies for delegating tasks, leaders can cultivate a collaborative work environment where each team member operates at their best. This subpoint will delve into key elements of effective delegation, including task analysis, providing clear instructions, maintaining regular check-ins, and establishing a feedback loop.

Task Analysis: Matching Tasks to Team Members

The first step in effective delegation is task analysis. You must assess each task to determine the most suitable team member for the job. This involves understanding the strengths, skills, and development goals of your team. For instance, if a task requires advanced technical skills, it should be assigned to someone who excels in that area. Conversely, routine tasks can be delegated to less experienced team members, allowing them to build their skills gradually.

Task analysis is not just about matching skills; it's also about considering each team member's workload and career aspirations. If an employee has expressed interest in project management, assigning them a small leadership role can help them gain valuable experience. This practice not only ensures tasks are completed efficiently but also supports the professional growth of your team members.

Clear Instructions: Setting Your Team Up for Success

Once tasks are assigned, it's crucial to provide clear instructions. Ambiguity can lead to misunderstandings, errors, and frustration. When delegating, take the time to explain the expectations, desired outcomes, and any deadlines. Clearly outline what success looks like and provide any necessary resources or tools required to complete the task.

Clear instructions should also include an explanation of the task's relevance. Understanding how their work contributes to the larger goals of the organization can motivate team members and give them a sense of purpose. It's helpful to use specific examples or previous successful projects as benchmarks.

Providing concise and thorough instructions upfront can minimize confusion and reduce the need for constant supervision. It sets a solid foundation for task execution and allows team members to work independently, increasing efficiency and trust within the team (Forbes, 2023).

Regular Check-ins: Keeping Communication Open

Regular check-ins are essential for maintaining open communication and offering support during task execution. These meetings provide an opportunity to address any questions or challenges that may arise. They ensure that the team stays aligned with the project's goals and timelines.

Establishing a consistent schedule for check-ins, such as weekly or biweekly meetings, can help maintain momentum and keep everyone accountable. During these sessions, focus on progress updates, identify any obstacles, and discuss potential solutions. Encouraging an open dialogue fosters a supportive environment where team members feel comfortable sharing their concerns and seeking help when needed.

Check-ins should strike a balance between staying informed and avoiding micromanagement. Rather than dictating every step, ask open-ended questions that prompt team members to reflect on their progress and share their insights. This approach not only builds trust but also empowers team members to take ownership of their tasks.

Feedback Loop: Ensuring Completion to Satisfaction

Establishing a feedback loop is critical to ensuring that tasks are completed to satisfaction. Feedback is a two-way street; it involves both providing constructive feedback to your team members and being open to receiving their input. This process helps refine future delegation practices and enhances overall team performance.

When providing feedback, be specific and focus on both strengths and areas for improvement. Acknowledge the efforts and achievements of your team members, and offer actionable suggestions for any shortcomings. Positive reinforcement boosts morale and encourages continued excellence, while constructive criticism fosters growth and development.

> **Success Strategy**: Always approach the person you're giving feedback to the same way you'd want to be offered feedback.

Equally important is soliciting feedback from your team. Encourage them to share their experiences and insights on the delegation process. Ask questions such as, *What could have been done differently?* or *How can I better support you in future tasks?* This collaborative approach builds trust and demonstrates that you value their perspectives. Creating a culture of continuous feedback promotes accountability and drives improvements across the team. It ensures that tasks are completed effectively and aligns efforts with the organization's goals.

Building Trust With Your Team

In leadership, trust is the cornerstone of any successful relationship and team dynamic. Leaders who prioritize trust create an environment where team members feel valued, engaged, and motivated to perform their best.

Trust begins with the leader's authenticity. Authenticity involves being genuine in interactions, showing your true self, and aligning actions with core values. When leaders are authentic, they foster trust and credibility. This means acknowledging your strengths and weaknesses and sharing personal experiences that highlight your human side.

Transparency is another vital element in building trust within a team. Transparency involves communicating openly and honestly about company matters, project status, and decision-making processes. By sharing information candidly, leaders foster a culture where employees feel included and aware of what's happening. Regular updates, whether through meetings or newsletters, can help keep everyone informed. Encouraging open communication also means creating a safe space where team members can express their opinions and ideas without fear of retribution. Leaders must be approachable and willing to listen, making team members feel heard and valued.

Consistency in actions and decisions plays a significant role in establishing trustworthiness. Consistency ensures that you follow through on your promises and commitments. Team members are more likely to trust leaders who demonstrate predictable behavior and steady decision-making processes.

For example, if you consistently recognizes hard work and rewards it, team members will trust that their efforts will be acknowledged. On the other hand, inconsistency breeds uncertainty and doubt, eroding trust over time.

Accountability is crucial in trust-building. You should hold yourself accountable for your actions and decisions. By taking responsibility, you set a powerful example for your team members. Accountability involves admitting mistakes, learning from them, and being transparent about how such errors will be addressed. When you take ownership of your actions, you encourage a culture of accountability within the team. Team members will feel more comfortable owning up to their mistakes, knowing that it's a part of the growth process rather than a cause for punishment.

> **Success Strategy**: You're a leader and that means you cannot demand anything from your team members that you don't expect of yourself. It starts with you. Stop and identify five key behaviors (including accountability) you want yourself and your team to live up to.

Being authentic in leadership requires self-awareness. You need to understand your values, strengths, and areas for improvement. Self-awareness helps you connect better with your team members as they understand how their actions and words impact others. It allows leaders to communicate more effectively and show empathy, which is essential for nurturing trust. Showing vulnerability is also a part of authenticity. When you share your challenges and failures, they become more relatable and approachable. This openness breaks down barriers and fosters stronger connections with team members.

To maintain consistency, you should establish clear guidelines and standards that guide your actions and decisions. These standards should reflect the organization's values and goals. By adhering to these guidelines consistently, leaders build a reputation for reliability and fairness. For example, if an organization values innovation, the leader should consistently encourage and reward creative solutions. Over time, this consistent behavior reinforces trust among team members, as they can predict and rely on the leader's actions. Another aspect of trust-building is recognizing and rewarding accountability and responsible behavior within the team. Celebrating successes and acknowledging those who take ownership of their tasks reinforce positive behaviors. Recognition doesn't always have to be grand gestures; even simple acknowledgments in meetings or through emails can significantly boost morale. This practice not only builds trust but also motivates others to follow suit.

Building trust through authenticity, transparency, consistency, and accountability creates a solid foundation for effective leadership. These elements intertwine to foster an environment where team members feel secure, respected, and empowered. As trust grows, so does collaboration, creativity, and overall team performance. By prioritizing trust, leaders can navigate the complexities of leadership with confidence and drive their teams toward success.

Fostering Accountability

Accountability in leadership is foundational for creating a thriving and effective team. When you hold yourself and your team members accountable, it builds a culture of trust, responsibility, and high performance. To cultivate such an environment, there are several key strategies that leaders can implement.

Setting Expectations

The first step in fostering accountability within your team is setting clear expectations. Leaders must articulate the specific responsibilities and goals for each team member. This clarity eliminates ambiguity and ensures that everyone understands what is expected of them.

It's essential to make sure these expectations are communicated transparently and consistently reviewed and updated to reflect any changes in priorities or goals. This practice not only keeps the team aligned but also reinforces the importance of accountability in daily operations.

Feedback Mechanisms

Implementing effective feedback mechanisms is another critical aspect of nurturing accountability. Regular and constructive feedback helps track progress, identify areas for improvement, and address issues before they escalate. Establishing routine check-ins or performance reviews can provide structured opportunities for this feedback. During these sessions, leaders should focus on both positive achievements and areas needing development, ensuring a balanced approach. Feedback should be specific, actionable, and delivered promptly to be most effective. Additionally, creating safe channels for peer feedback encourages open communication within the team. Anonymous surveys or group feedback sessions can help team members share honest observations without fear of retribution. These mechanisms create an environment where continuous improvement is valued and everyone feels accountable for their contributions and growth.

Recognition of Efforts

Recognizing and rewarding responsible behavior and accountability within the team is crucial for reinforcing these values. When team members see that their hard work and commitment are acknowledged, it motivates them to maintain high standards. Recognition can come in various forms, from public praise during team meetings to more formal awards or bonuses. It's important to celebrate both individual and collective achievements to foster a collaborative spirit. For instance, acknowledging a team member who goes above and beyond to meet a deadline or solve a problem can inspire others to follow suit. By making recognition a regular practice, leaders can build a positive and supportive culture where accountability is seen as a pathway to success rather than merely a requirement.

Learning From Mistakes

Encouraging a growth mindset within the team means viewing mistakes as learning opportunities rather than failures. This approach helps individuals feel safe to take risks and innovate, knowing that errors will be met with constructive feedback rather than blame. Remember, you play a crucial role in modeling this behavior by openly discussing your own mistakes and what they learned from them. This transparency fosters trust and shows that accountability includes owning up to and learning from one's missteps. When addressing mistakes within the team, it's important to focus on solutions and preventive measures rather than dwelling on the error itself. This can involve collaborative problem-solving sessions where team members discuss what went wrong and how similar issues can be avoided in the future. By promoting a culture that values learning and resilience, you can help your team become more adaptable and committed to continuous improvement.

Creating a Culture of Accountability

Building and maintaining a culture of accountability requires ongoing effort and dedication. You need to consistently reinforce the importance of accountability through your actions and policies. Providing clear guidelines for team conduct, facilitating open communication, and offering support are all part of this process. Regularly revisiting team goals and ensuring they remain relevant and achievable can keep everyone focused and motivated. Promoting a growth mindset and celebrating milestones, no matter how small, can contribute significantly to a positive and accountable team culture. As you model these behaviors and principles, your team is more likely to embrace and uphold the same standards, leading to a more cohesive and high-performing organization.

Bringing It All Together

Throughout this chapter, we have explored the significance of mastering delegation and building trust within your team. Effective delegation not only empowers team members but also enhances overall efficiency by allowing leaders to focus on strategic tasks. By sharing responsibilities and providing clear instructions, leaders can foster a culture where everyone feels valued and motivated.

This sense of ownership leads to increased confidence and proactive problem-solving, essential traits for a successful team. Building trust requires authenticity, transparency, consistency, and accountability. When you are genuine in your interactions and openly communicate expectations, you create an environment where team members feel secure and respected. Regular check-ins and constructive feedback ensure that everyone stays aligned with the organization's goals while promoting growth and continuous improvement. By prioritizing these elements, leaders can cultivate a strong, collaborative, and high-performing team that is well-equipped to tackle any challenge.

In the last chapter of this book, we'll be looking at why a lifelong commitment to improvement is vital for your growth as a leader. Embracing continuous education is the road to leading with confidence and innovation. So, let's look at how you can continue to navigate the complexities of the modern business environment successfully.

Chapter 10:
Lifelong Learning and Continuous Improvement

What I always say is, 'Do every job you're in like you're going to do it for the rest of your life, and demonstrate that ownership of it.' –Mary Barra

As trends and technologies rapidly change, staying up-to-date through the acquisition of new skills becomes crucial, especially for women who are aiming for leadership roles. This chapter delves into the importance of embracing continuous education.

In this chapter, you will discover how continuous learning fuels innovation and creativity, vital components for successful problem-solving and leadership. Various methods such as attending workshops, seminars, and webinars will be explored as effective ways to stay informed and inspired. Additionally, we will discuss the positive impact of continuous education on personal development, including boosting confidence and self-esteem. By committing to lifelong learning, you can better handle uncertainties and set an inspiring example for your teams, fostering a culture where growth and adaptability flourish.

Embracing Continuous Education

Acquiring new skills is a cornerstone of continuous education. In the corporate world and entrepreneurial ventures, staying relevant is crucial as trends and technologies evolve rapidly. Embracing new skills equips you with the tools you need to adapt to these changes effectively. Leaders who invest in learning about emerging technologies such as artificial intelligence or blockchain can steer their organizations toward innovative strategies and stay ahead of competitors.

This adaptability ensures that you are not just responding to changes but actively shaping the future. Continuous learning goes beyond merely acquiring new skills; it fosters innovation and creativity, essential ingredients for successful problem-solving. When you expose yourself to diverse fields of knowledge, you develop a more robust toolkit for tackling challenges. For instance, a leader well-versed in design thinking may approach organizational issues differently than one trained traditionally in business strategies. This unique perspective can lead to creative solutions that others might overlook, driving the organization forward. By cultivating a culture of continuous learning, you encourage your team to think outside the box, promoting an environment where innovation thrives.

Learning new things isn't just beneficial for professional development; it also boosts confidence and self-esteem. Women in leadership positions face unique challenges, such as overcoming gender biases and balancing work-life responsibilities. Continuous education can empower you to navigate these obstacles more effectively. For instance, mastering public speaking through a dedicated course can help you feel more confident when presenting ideas to stakeholders, thereby enhancing your influence and credibility.

> **Success Strategy**: It's challenging to study when you have a full-time job, but don't let that discourage you. Embrace technology and use e-learning platforms that provide you with flexible learning opportunities.

The journey of continuous learning aligns closely with the principles of adaptability and resilience. Leaders who commit to lifelong learning can better handle the uncertainties and complexities inherent in modern business environments. For instance, during economic downturns, a well-informed leader might pivot their business strategy to focus on emerging markets or develop new product lines that cater to shifting consumer preferences. This adaptability is not only about surviving but thriving in adverse conditions, turning potential setbacks into opportunities for growth. Moreover, resilient leaders set an example for their teams, cultivating a workforce that's prepared to innovate and excel, regardless of external pressures. Networking and collaboration are integral to the continuous learning journey. Engaging with peers and experts in one's field opens doors to new ideas and partnerships that can drive innovation. For example, joining a professional association or community group related to one's industry provides access to a wealth of knowledge and experiences shared by others. These interactions often spark novel ideas and collaborations that can lead to breakthrough developments. Networking also exposes you to different perspectives, broadening your understanding and enabling you to make more comprehensive and inclusive decisions.

Seeking Feedback for Growth

Feedback plays a pivotal role in the continuous cycle of personal and professional development. By embracing constructive feedback, you can identify areas for enhancement and cultivate your skills more effectively. In both corporate settings and entrepreneurial ventures, the ability to receive and apply feedback is instrumental in advancing one's career and fostering leadership capabilities.

Constructive feedback serves as a mirror, reflecting not only an individual's strengths but also the areas needing improvement. For instance, receiving constructive criticism on presentation skills can highlight a lack of confidence or clarity in communication. Addressing such feedback can lead to targeted efforts aimed at refining these essential abilities. This process of acknowledging weaknesses and working toward improvement is fundamental to personal growth and skill development.

Seeking feedback from a variety of sources is equally crucial. Feedback from mentors, colleagues, and team members provides a spectrum of perspectives that enriches the learning experience. Mentors, with their wealth of experience, can offer invaluable insights into industry-specific nuances and long-term career strategies. Colleagues can provide immediate and practical advice on daily tasks and interactions. Team members' feedback brings another dimension, often highlighting aspects of teamwork, collaboration, and project management. Together, these diverse viewpoints create a comprehensive picture, enabling a more thorough self-assessment and facilitating well-rounded development.

Once feedback is received, it is essential to set actionable goals based on this information. For example, if feedback reveals you have a tendency to dominate conversations in meetings, you could set a goal of improving your active listening skills by consciously allowing others to speak first and engaging more attentively.

> **Success Strategy**: Effective leaders constantly evolve by listening to the people around them.

To illustrate the impact of feedback on leadership practices, consider a scenario where a leader receives feedback regarding their need to improve decision-making transparency. Acting on this, the leader might start sharing more information about the decision-making process during team meetings. This change can foster greater trust among team members and, over time, build a more collaborative and transparent work culture. Such improvements not only benefit the leader personally but also enhance the overall effectiveness of the organization.

Another example can be seen in entrepreneurs who actively seek customer feedback to refine their products or services. By listening to their customers' needs and preferences, they can make informed adjustments, thereby increasing customer satisfaction and business success. This iterative process of feedback and improvement is crucial for staying competitive in the market.

Staying Current With Industry Trends

Staying updated on industry trends is crucial for leadership effectiveness. In today's fast-paced world, you must continually educate yourself to remain relevant and make well-informed decisions. By understanding the latest developments in your field, you can craft strategic plans that align with current realities and future projections. This knowledge equips you to anticipate changes, mitigate risks, and seize opportunities promptly.

One practical way to stay informed is through subscribing to industry publications, newsletters, and reports. These resources provide valuable insights and updates on market movements, technological advancements, regulatory changes, and competitor activities. For instance, a leader in the tech industry might follow publications like Wired or TechCrunch to understand emerging technologies and market shifts. Regularly consuming these updates helps leaders maintain a current and thorough understanding of their industry, enabling them to make decisions backed by up-to-date information.

Embracing change and innovation is another vital aspect of staying competitive and relevant. The business landscape is continuously evolving, driven by advancements in technology, shifts in consumer behavior, and global economic changes. Leaders who resist change risk falling behind, while those who embrace and drive innovation position themselves and their organizations for sustained success. An example of this can be seen in the retail industry, where companies like Amazon have consistently innovated in areas such as logistics, customer service, and product offerings, thereby maintaining their edge over competitors.

Continuous research and learning are fundamental practices that underpin the ability to adapt to and capitalize on industry trends. You should allocate time for regular study and exploration of new concepts, tools, and practices.

Personal Development Strategies

Regular self-reflection is a cornerstone of personal growth. It plays a critical role in enhancing self-awareness and emotional intelligence—two qualities vital for effective leadership. Through self-reflection, you can examine your actions, motivations, and reactions in various scenarios. This introspection allows you to understand your strengths and areas needing improvement, ultimately leading to more informed and empathetic decision-making. For instance, a leader who regularly reflects on her interactions with her team might notice that her communication style could be more inclusive, prompting her to make necessary adjustments.

By fostering self-awareness, self-reflection also helps leaders maintain emotional balance, even in high-pressure situations. Setting clear, precise goals ensures that leaders have a roadmap for their growth journey. For example, rather than vaguely aiming to "improve communication skills," a leader might set a SMART goal like "complete a professional communication course within six months and apply learned techniques in monthly team meetings." Such goals not only provide direction but also enable leaders to track their progress and celebrate small victories along the way. Regularly reviewing and adjusting these goals based on feedback and experiences further ensures that leaders stay aligned with their long-term vision.

> **Success Strategy**: Adaptability is key to success in a constantly changing environment. When you're able to adjust your goals, you demonstrate your commitment to continuous improvement and growth of your team and the organization.

Finally, it is important to recognize that personal development in leadership roles is a lifelong journey. There will always be new skills to acquire, challenges to overcome, and opportunities for growth. Embracing this mindset encourages leaders to remain curious, open-minded, and resilient. For instance, a female entrepreneur might continuously seek out new business trends, technological advancements, and market opportunities to stay ahead in her industry. By committing to ongoing learning and self-improvement, leaders can adapt to changing circumstances, innovate, and inspire others.

Final Thoughts

Committing to lifelong learning is essential for staying relevant and successful in today's rapidly changing world. By continually acquiring new skills and knowledge, women aspiring toward leadership roles can adapt to evolving trends and technologies. This adaptability allows them not only to respond to changes but also to shape the future of their industries. Leaders who embrace continuous education become innovators, equipped with fresh perspectives and creative problem-solving abilities. Their commitment to learning fosters an environment where their teams can thrive, encouraging everyone to think outside the box and drive progress. Networking and seeking feedback are crucial components of this journey. Engaging with peers, mentors, and industry experts provides valuable insights and opens doors to new opportunities. Constructive criticism helps leaders identify areas for improvement, guiding their personal and professional growth. Setting clear goals and tracking progress ensure that their learning efforts are structured and purposeful. By embracing a mindset of continuous improvement, you can confidently navigate challenges, inspire your team, and achieve sustained success in both corporate settings and entrepreneurial ventures.

Conclusion

As we bring this journey to a close, it's essential to reflect on the new skills and insights you gained in your leadership development. Each step covered in this book provides a piece of the puzzle that makes up an effective and inspiring leader. Now, as you stand at the threshold of applying these lessons to your own career, there are a few key insights to keep at the forefront of your mind.

First, let's consider the power of emotional intelligence. The best leaders aren't just those who can strategize or make tough decisions; they are those who understand their team members on a fundamental level. Imagine a scenario where a team member is grappling with personal issues. Your ability to empathize, to feel what they are feeling, not only offers them support but also fortifies the bond within the team. This empathetic approach ensures that your team feels valued and understood, leading to a more motivated and cohesive working environment. When you navigate emotions—both yours and others'—with skill, you create a ripple effect of positivity and productivity that permeates every aspect of the workplace.

Equally important is the cultivation of strong relationships grounded in trust and mutual respect. The corporate landscape is littered with tales of projects gone awry due to lack of collaboration or understanding among colleagues. Think of a time when a colleague stood by you during a particularly challenging project. I'm sure you'd agree that the trust that such experiences build is invaluable. It transforms ordinary coworkers into steadfast allies who are willing to go the extra mile for collective success. This network of trusted relationships becomes your pillar of support, allowing you to tackle challenges head-on with confidence and resilience. Furthermore, mastering the art of effective delegation can significantly enhance your leadership repertoire. Leadership isn't about shouldering all responsibilities alone; it's about recognizing the strengths and potential within your team and leveraging them appropriately. By entrusting your team with important duties, you empower them to develop their skills and take ownership of their work. This approach not only lightens your load but also fosters a culture of accountability and growth within the team. Finally, never underestimate the power of continuous growth and learning in your journey as a leader. The business world is ever-evolving, with new challenges and opportunities emerging continually. A commitment to lifelong learning keeps you at the cutting edge of industry trends and equips you with innovative solutions to propel your organization forward. Envision a future where your dedication to pushing boundaries with creative ideas not only benefits your immediate team but also sets a precedent for excellence and ambition across the board. Staying curious, open-minded, and adaptable positions you as a visionary leader capable of navigating the complexities of modern business environments.

In closing, remember that leadership is not a destination but an ongoing journey. It's about consistently applying these principles—emotional intelligence, building strong relationships, effective delegation, and continuous growth—in your daily interactions and decision-making processes. The landscape may shift, and the challenges may vary, but with these foundational elements, you are well-equipped to rise to any occasion with optimism and grace.

Your path forward is filled with promise and potential. Embrace each opportunity as a chance to demonstrate the powerful leader you have become. As you navigate the complexities of corporate settings or steer your entrepreneurial ventures, let these insights guide you toward creating inclusive, empowering, and forward-thinking environments.

Leadership is a dynamic and transformative experience. It requires a balance of introspection and action, empathy, and decisiveness. You now possess the tools to lead with confidence and the wisdom to know that true leadership is as much about lifting others as it is about achieving your own goals. Embrace this responsibility with enthusiasm and an unwavering belief in the positive impact you can make.

Thank you for embarking on this journey and committing to your growth as a leader. As you move forward, carry these lessons with you, and remember that your ability to lead effectively lies within your capacity to inspire, connect, delegate, and innovate. Here's to your continued success and to the bright future you are poised to create.

References

10 Tips for Effective Networking. (n.d.). Careers.umbc.edu. https://careers.umbc.edu/students/network/networking101/tips/

5 Reasons High Performance Teams Need A Growth Mindset | Continued Learning. (n.d.). Continuedlearning.njit.edu. Retrieved July 24, 2024, from https://continuedlearning.njit.edu/5-reasons-high-performance-teams-need-growth-mindset

7 Benefits of Mentorship in Leadership - Support Services Group. (2023, March 10). Supportservicesgroup.co. https://supportservicesgroup.co/insights/benefits-of-mentorship-leadership/

7 Effective Networking Strategies for Business Students | Eller College of Management. (2024, February 20). Eller.arizona.edu. https://eller.arizona.edu/news/7-effective-networking-strategies-business-students

7 Unique Strengths Women Bring to the Table. (2024, March 18). Mahara Mindfulness. https://www.maharamindfulness.com/internationalwomensday/

Aldridge, E. (2023, October 18). What Is Leadership Training? Why Is It Important? Educate 360 Professional Training Partners. https://educate360.com/blog/leadership-training-for-employees/

American Battle Field Trust. (n.d.). Abigail Adams to John Adams - "Remember The Ladies".

https://www.battlefields.org/learn/primary-sources/abigail-adams-john-adams-remember-ladies

Amic, J. (2023, August 18). Leadership Traits in Women. MasterStart. https://masterstart.com/blog/women-leaders/exploring-common-and-underrated-leadership-traits-in-women/

Ariella, S. (2023). Women in leadership statistics: Facts on the gender gap in corporate and political leadership. Zippia. https://www.zippia.com/advice/women-in-leadership-statistics/

Bentley University. (2018). 7 Ways to Promote Diversity in the Workplace | Bentley University. Bentley University. https://www.bentley.edu/news/7-ways-promote-diversity-workplace

Bonterre, M. (2023, November 30). Empathetic Leadership: How to Go Beyond Lip Service - Harvard. Harvard Business Publishing. https://www.harvardbusiness.org/empathetic-leadership-how-to-go-beyond-lip-service/

Bradley, J. (2023, July 9). The Art of Embracing Failure: Learning and Growing from Setbacks. Lampshade of ILLUMINATION. https://medium.com/lampshade-of-illumination/the-art-of-embracing-failure-learning-and-growing-from-setbacks-af7a6dbe6b5c

Bump in the road: How insights professionals can learn from setbacks | Feature. (n.d.). Research Live. Retrieved July 24, 2024, from https://www.research-live.com/article/features/bump-in-the-road-how-insights-professionals-can-learn-from-setbacks/id/5123152

Burkett, E. (2019). Women's rights movement - Successes and failures. Encyclopædia Britannica.

https://www.britannica.com/event/womens-movement/Successes-and-failures

Camarote, R. (2023). How to tune into your nonverbal leadership signals. Inc.com. https://www.inc.com/robin-camarote/how-to-tune-into-your-non-verbal-leadership-signals.html

Catalyst. (2022). Women in management: Quick take. https://www.catalyst.org/research/women-in-management/

Center for Creative Leadership. (2023). The importance of empathy in the workplace. https://www.ccl.org/articles/leading-effectively-articles/empathy-in-the-workplace-a-tool-for-effective-leadership/

Coach, S. B. R. L. (2022, December 5). Why Imposter Syndrome Affects Female Leaders More Than Men. Real Life Resilience. https://medium.com/real-life-resilience/why-imposter-syndrome-affects-female-leaders-more-than-men-962abcea8983

Continuous Learning: The Lifelong Journey of Leadership Skills. (2023, October 25). The Economic Times. https://m.economictimes.com/jobs/c-suite/continuous-learning-the-lifelong-journey-of-leadership-skills/articleshow/104702641.cms

Cuncic, A. (2024, February 12). 7 Active listening techniques for better communication. Verywell Mind. https://www.verywellmind.com/what-is-active-listening-3024343

Davaei, M., Gunkel, M., Veglio, V., & Taras, V. (2022, June). The influence of cultural intelligence and emotional intelligence on conflict occurrence and performance in global virtual teams.

Journal of International Management. https://doi.org/10.1016/j.intman.2022.100969

De Bruycker, I. & McLoughlin, A. (2020,). The public affairs plan: Seven steps to success rooted in science and practice. *Journal of Public Affairs.* https://doi.org/10.1002/pa.2567

De Smet, A., Gast, A., Lavoie, J., & Lurie, M. (2023, May 4). New Leadership for a New Era of Thriving Organizations | McKinsey. Www.mckinsey.com. https://www.mckinsey.com/capabilities/people-and-organizational-performance/our-insights/new-leadership-for-a-new-era-of-thriving-organizations

Dixon-Fyle, S., Dolan, K., Hunt, V. & Prince, S. (2019). Diversity wins: How inclusion matters. McKinsey and Company. https://www.mckinsey.com/featured-insights/diversity-and-inclusion/diversity-wins-how-inclusion-matters#/

Eleanor Roosevelt quote. Good Reads. https://www.goodreads.com/quotes/3823-you-gain-strength-courage-and-confidence-by-every-experience-in

Elias, E. (2018, March 12). Lessons learned from women in leadership positions. Work. https://doi.org/10.3233/wor-172675

Elliot, K. (2023). Why mentorship is even more important when you're a leader. Forbes. https://www.forbes.com/sites/forbescoachescouncil/2023/02/24/why-mentorship-is-even-more-important-when-youre-a-leader/

Emerson, M. (2022). Women negotiation skills. Harvard DCE. https://professional.dce.harvard.edu/blog/women-negotiation-skills-how-women-can-get-what-they-want-in-a-negotiation/

Equal Rights Advocates. (2019). Gender Discrimination at Work - Equal Rights Advocates. Equal Rights Advocates; Equal Rights Advocates. https://www.equalrights.org/issue/economic-workplace-equality/discrimination-at-work/

Fighting Gender Bias. (2022, May 5). AWIS. https://awis.org/fighting-gender-bias/

Forbes. (2023). How to delegate effectively: 8 Ways to make the most of your team's time and talent. https://www.forbes.com/sites/allbusiness/2023/05/25/how-to-delegate-effectively-8-ways-to-make-the-most-of-your-teams-time-and-talent/

Froehlicher, M., Griek, L. K., Nematzadeh, A., Hall, L., & Stovall, N. (2021, February 5). Gender equality in the workplace: going beyond women on the board. S&P Global. https://www.spglobal.com/esg/csa/yearbook/articles/gender-equality-workplace-going-beyond-women-on-the-board

Gavin, M. (2019, November 27). 5 Steps to Creating a Successful Leadership Development Plan. Business Insights - Blog; Harvard Business School. https://online.hbs.edu/blog/post/leadership-development-plan

Gender Equality • Business & Human Rights Navigator. (n.d.). Business & Human Rights Navigator. https://bhr-navigator.unglobalcompact.org/issues/gender-equality/

Grossman, D. (2023, July 17). The Benefits of Delegation and Why Most Leaders Under-Delegate. Www.yourthoughtpartner.com.

https://www.yourthoughtpartner.com/blog/the-benefits-of-delegation-and-why-most-leaders-under-delegate

Grossmann, C. (2022, August 22). 5 Ways to Promote Workplace Diversity Through Employee Engagement. Beekeeper. https://www.beekeeper.io/blog/5-ways-promote-workplace-diversity/

Gunkel, M., Schlaegel, C., & Taras, V. (2016). Cultural values, emotional intelligence, and conflict handling styles: A global study. Journal of World Business.

Harrison, M., Tran, D. N., Pena, A., Iyengar, S., Ahmed Abubakar, A., Hoernke, K., John-Akinola, Y. O., Kiplagat, S., Marconi, A. M., Vaghaiwalla, T. M., Kalbarczyk, A., & Weinberg, J. L. (2022). Strategies to Improve Women's Leadership Preparation for Early Career Global Health Professionals: Suggestions from Two Working Groups. Annals of Global Health. https://doi.org/10.5334/aogh.3705

Hasanagic, A. (2019, November 2). 25 Organizations Fighting for Gender Equality | Human Rights Careers. Human Rights Careers. https://www.humanrightscareers.com/magazine/organizations-gender-equality/

Hastwell, C. (2023). Creating a culture of recognition. Great Place to Work. https://www.greatplacetowork.com/resources/blog/creating-a-culture-of-recognition

HeforShe. (n.d.). UN Women. https://www.heforshe.org/en

How to Motivate Employees Through the Power of Positive Leadership. (n.d.). Www.coffeepals.com. Retrieved July 24, 2024, from https://www.coffeepals.com/blog/how-to-motivate-employees-through-the-power-of-positive-leadership

How women can negotiate for more. (n.d.). Lean In. https://leanin.org/negotiation

Ibarra, H., & Hunter, M. L. (2007, January). How Leaders Create and Use Networks. Harvard Business Review. https://hbr.org/2007/01/how-leaders-create-and-use-networks

Inc, G. (2023). Mentors and sponsors make the difference. Gallup.com. https://www.gallup.com/workplace/473999/mentors-sponsors-difference.aspx

Jones, M. (2024, July 1). Strategic planning: How to set and meet your long-term goals. Blog Wrike. https://www.wrike.com/blog/strategic-planning/

Kalev, A. & Dobbin, F. (2022). The surprising benefits of work/life support. Harvard Business Review. https://hbr.org/2022/09/the-surprising-benefits-of-work-life-support

Khan, R., & Ltd, P. M. M. P. (2023, May 12). How imposter syndrome hurts women leaders. People Matters. https://www.peoplematters.in/article/leadership/how-imposter-syndrome-hurts-women-leaders-37127

Kleynhans, D. J., Heyns, M. M., Stander, M. W., & de Beer, L. T. (2022). Authentic leadership, trust (in the leader), and flourishing: Does precariousness matter? Frontiers in Psychology. https://doi.org/10.3389/fpsyg.2022.798759

Landry, L. (2019). Why emotional intelligence is important in leadership. Harvard Business School Online.

https://online.hbs.edu/blog/post/emotional-intelligence-in-leadership

Landry, L. (2020, January 14). How to Delegate Effectively: 7 Tips for Managers. Harvard Business School Online. https://online.hbs.edu/blog/post/how-to-delegate-effectively

Larralde, A. (2023, June 16). Accountability in Leadership. Betterworks. https://www.betterworks.com/magazine/accountability-in-leadership/

Leadership strategies to develop and utilize emotional intelligence | Thunderbird. (n.d.). Thunderbird.asu.edu. https://thunderbird.asu.edu/thought-leadership/insights/leadership-strategies-develop-and-utilize-emotional-intelligence

Lewis, A. (2022, October 26). Good leadership? It all starts with trust. Harvard Business Publishing. https://www.harvardbusiness.org/good-leadership-it-all-starts-with-trust/

Marsh, E. (2019, January 29). Personal development and the power of feedback. T-Three. https://www.t-three.com/thinking-space/blog/personal-development-and-the-power-of-feedback

Maven: The Key to High-Performing Teams: Cultivating Accountability. (n.d.). Maven.com. https://maven.com/articles/build-a-culture-of-accountability

Mayo Clinic. (2022, July 6). 7 steps to boost your self-esteem. Mayo Clinic. https://www.mayoclinic.org/healthy-lifestyle/adult-health/in-depth/self-esteem/art-20045374

Mesquita, R. (2024). The power of persuasive leadership. Millenia Atlantic University. www.maufl.edu.

https://www.maufl.edu/en/news-and-events/macaws-blog/persuasive-leadership

Mind Tools Content Team. (2022). MindTools | Home. Www.mindtools.com. https://www.mindtools.com/ax3c2aw/celebrating-achievement

Moldoveanu, M., & Narayandas, D. (2019, April). The Future of Leadership Development. Harvard Business Review; hbr.org. https://hbr.org/2019/03/the-future-of-leadership-development

North, M. (2020, March 17). 10 Tips for Improving Your Public Speaking Skills. Professional Development | Harvard DCE; Harvard University. https://professional.dce.harvard.edu/blog/10-tips-for-improving-your-public-speaking-skills/

Page Personnel. (n.d.). The value of mentorship and sponsorship, and what it can do for your company. https://www.pagepersonnel.com.au/advice/career-and-management/career-progression/value-of-mentorship-and-sponsorship

Penn LPS. (2023, August 9). Why communication is essential to effective leadership. Lpsonline.sas.upenn.edu. https://lpsonline.sas.upenn.edu/features/why-communication-essential-effective-leadership

Rampton, K. (2019). 50 Motivational quotes from inspiring women leaders. Entrepreneur.

https://www.entrepreneur.com/leadership/50-motivational-quotes-from-inspiring-women-leaders-like/300288

Resilience of the Human Spirit: Seizing Every Moment. (n.d.). ReVista. https://revista.drclas.harvard.edu/resilience-of-the-human-spirit-seizing-every-moment/

Robinson, L., & Smith, M. (2023, October 11). Stress Management. HelpGuide. https://www.helpguide.org/articles/stress/stress-management.htm

Saint Leo University. (2021, May 28). 9 Tips to improve your public speaking skills | Saint Leo University. Www.saintleo.edu. https://www.saintleo.edu/about/stories/blog/9-tips-to-improve-your-public-speaking-skills

Scott, E. (2023, September 13). 18 Highly Effective Stress Relievers. Verywell Mind; Verywellmind. https://www.verywellmind.com/tips-to-reduce-stress-3145195

Slåtten, T., Mutonyi, B. R., & Lien, G. (2021, May 21). Does Organizational Vision Really matter? an Empirical Examination of Factors Related to Organizational Vision Integration among Hospital Employees. BMC Health Services Research. https://doi.org/10.1186/s12913-021-06503-3

Stobierski, T. (2019). How leaders develop and use their network. Harvard Business School Online. https://online.hbs.edu/blog/post/importance-of-networking-in-leadership

The Importance of Delegation for Leadership. (n.d.). Eagle's Flight. https://www.eaglesflight.com/resource/the-importance-of-delegation-for-leadership/

The Importance of Feedback for Personal and Professional Growth - HR Future. (2023, April 11). Www.hrfuture.net.

https://www.hrfuture.net/talent-management/training-development/the-importance-of-feedback-for-personal-and-professional-growth/

The Importance of Influencing Skills and How to Improve Them. (2023). University of Minnesota. https://ccaps.umn.edu/story/importance-influencing-skills-and-how-improve-them

Toward a Coalitional Identity. (n.d.). BlackStar. Retrieved July 24, 2024, from https://www.blackstarfest.org/seen/read/issue-001/toward-a-coalitional-identity/

UN Women. (2023, September 18). Facts and Figures: Leadership and Political Participation. UN Women; United Nations. https://www.unwomen.org/en/what-we-do/leadership-and-political-participation/facts-and-figures

Wallis, A. (2020, March 4). How to Create a Personal Growth and Professional Development Plan. Www.snhu.edu. https://www.snhu.edu/about-us/newsroom/career/personal-development-plan

Wedgwood, J. (2019, August 29). The Importance of Work-Life Balance | The Happiness Index. Thehappinessindex.com. https://thehappinessindex.com/blog/importance-work-life-balance

Wells, R. (2023, October 31). 5 Ways To Show Your Visionary Leadership Skills. Forbes. https://www.forbes.com/sites/rachelwells/2023/10/31/5-ways-to-show-your-visionary-leadership-skills/

Westover, J. H. (2023, October 31). Building Stronger Relationships at Work: The Power of Effective Listening. HCI Consulting.

https://www.innovativehumancapital.com/post/building-stronger-relationships-at-work-the-power-of-effective-listening

Whitenight, S. L. (2024, February 12). Strategic Planning and Goal Setting in Business Operations Management. Medium. https://medium.com/@LatinaBytes/strategic-planning-and-goal-setting-in-business-operations-management-025ba6d44a76

Willige, A. (2023, May 2). More than DEI: Why it pays to get women in the boardroom. World Economic Forum. https://www.weforum.org/agenda/2023/05/women-board-directors-dei-profitability/

Women's Empowerment Principles. (n.d.). https://www.weps.org/

World Economic Forum. (2022, July 13). Global Gender Gap Report 2022. World Economic Forum. https://www.weforum.org/publications/global-gender-gap-report-2022/in-full/2-4-gender-gaps-in-leadership-by-industry-and-cohort/

World Economic Forum. (2024). Global gender gap report 2024. https://www.weforum.org/publications/global-gender-gap-report-2024/digest/

Worthen, M. (2020). The women's rights movement and the women of Seneca Falls. https://www.biography.com/activists/seneca-falls-convention-leaders

Yousef Farhan, B. (2024, June 1). Visionary leadership and innovative mindset for sustainable business development: Case studies and practical applications. Research in Globalization. https://doi.org/10.1016/j.resglo.2024.100219

Zasa, F. P., & Buganza, T. (2022). Developing a shared vision: strong teams have the power. Journal of Business Strategy, 44(6), 415-425. https://doi.org/10.1108/JBS-04-2022-0065

About The Author

Jess Pryce is the pen name of a distinguished manufacturing executive with an illustrious career spanning over 25 years. With an unwavering commitment to leadership excellence, Jess has made significant contributions to the business world since embarking on a remarkable journey in manufacturing in 1995.

Armed with an engineering bachelor's degree that laid the foundation for a deep understanding of the intricacies of industry, Jess went on to achieve an MBA that further honed expertise in management and leadership. Complementing this academic foundation, Jess holds coveted certificates in leadership, continuous improvement, and management, and proudly bears the title of CPIM certification.

The pursuit of knowledge and growth knows no bounds for Jess. Having successfully completed the Thunderbird-School of Global Management Executive Leadership Program, Jess has gained insights and perspectives that extend beyond conventional boundaries, reflecting an unparalleled dedication to personal and professional development.

Currently holding a prominent position in the C-suite of a thriving manufacturing enterprise, Jess seamlessly integrates theoretical acumen with real-world insights. This fusion of theory and practice, enriched by years of hands-on experience, forms the bedrock of Jess Pryce's authoritative works on leadership.

While the world might recognize Jess Pryce as a prolific author, the true essence of this journey lies in Jess's passion for knowledge dissemination. As an adjunct professor, Jess imparts wisdom in Operations Management at the Graduate level, shaping the minds of future leaders with practical insights and strategic thinking. This commitment to education stands as a testament to Jess's desire to give back to the community and empower the next generation of trailblazers.

It is essential to underscore that Jess Pryce is a pen name, deliberately chosen to preserve the focus on the realm where Jess's expertise truly shines – the world of manufacturing and executive leadership. As a dedicated C-suite executive, Jess's primary role remains at the forefront of business operations, steering companies toward innovation, growth, and success.

In the realm of authorship, Jess Pryce's contributions are a reflection of a seasoned leader's insights, wisdom, and devotion to advancing the field of leadership within the manufacturing landscape. While preferring to remain beyond the spotlight, Jess Pryce's impact reverberates through the pages of enlightening leadership books and within the halls of academia where future leaders are nurtured.

Additional Books by this Author

Jess Pryce has written and published the following books:

Leadership Series:

Leadership Coaching: Igniting Influence, Driving Innovation, and Cultivating Trust in Business

Leadership Coaching Official Companion Workbook

Leadership Coaching Discovery Journal

Leadership For Women: Resilient & Ready: Empowering Women to Lead With Confidence and Success

Leadership For Women: Resilient & Ready Official Companion Workbook

Leadership For Women: Resilient & Ready Discovery Journal

Accelerated Decision Making: The Art of Using the Executive Summary to Communicate Impacts, Recommendations, & Direction

Accelerated Decision Making Official Companion Workbook

Accelerated Decision Making Discovery Notebook

Watch for more books by this author!

(This page intentionally left blank)

Please Leave a Review on Amazon.com

www.ingramcontent.com/pod-product-compliance
Lightning Source LLC
Chambersburg PA
CBHW052300220526
45471CB00001B/422